I come in the flaming purity of the Christed ones. I come as the spokesman not only of the seven archangels, but also of the Lords of Karma and the seven chohans of the rays. For I come to fulfill the cosmic edict of the Lord "Behold, now is the accepted time: behold, now is the day of salvation." This day of days is the acceptable day of the Lord's judgment. And indeed judgment is meted out from the judgment seat. . . .

Now comes the great voice out of the temple speaking to the seven archangels, "Go your ways and pour out the vials of the wrath of God upon the earth." . . .

Therefore . . . I am come forth bearing the golden vial containing mankind's wrathful, most dreadful misuses of the sacred fire on the first ray of the will of God. . . .

And I come with deliverance to the nations and to the captives of the Luciferians; and I come to deliver the mandate of the Lord God—the mandate of mankind's own karma. Now let us see how the intensification of the sacred fire in the hearts of the devotees will be the all-consuming flame of the Holy Spirit that clears a pathway through the dark night of the soul over which the children of Israel may pass unto the light of the new day.

Archangel Michael

VIALS of the SEVEN LAST PLAGUES

The Judgments of Almighty God Delivered by The Seven Archangels

Dictated to the Messenger
Elizabeth Clare Prophet

Summit University Press®
Los Angeles

Vials of the Seven Last Plagues
Published by
SUMMIT UNIVERSITY PRESS

LIBRARY OF CONGRESS CATALOG CARD NUMBER: 76-28083

INTERNATIONAL STANDARD BOOK NUMBER: 0-916766-23-3

This book is set in 11 point Baskerville with 1 point lead

Printed in the United States of America

Third Printing

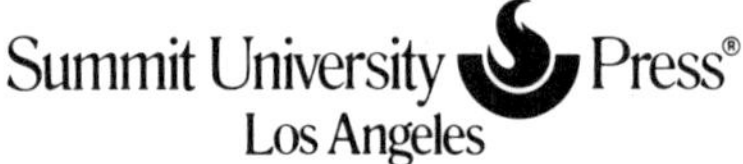

Cover: Oil painting by Norman Thomas Miller
Archangel Michael pouring out the first vial
of the wrath of God upon the earth.

God Is Speaking to His People

God is speaking to his people in this age as he has in all ages past. He speaks to their hearts and to their souls and he speaks to them through his prophets, teachers, and messengers whom he has sent to be the voice of the consciousness of Christ in the body of God on earth.

Vials of the Seven Last Plagues is the record of God's speaking to his people. It is the very pouring out of his Spirit upon his servants and his handmaids, which was spoken of by the prophet Joel. It is the setting forth of the judgments of the Great Law pronounced to this generation by the seven archangels, whose coming was foretold in the Revelation of Jesus Christ "sent and signified by his angel unto his servant John."

The fourteen messages contained in this book are the coming to pass of the signs recorded by Saint John the Divine in the fifteenth and sixteenth chapters of the Book of Revelation. They were dictated to Elizabeth Clare Prophet, messenger for the Great White Brotherhood, by the seven archangels and the seven archeiai in the same manner in which John received the Revelation of Jesus Christ, "which God gave unto him, to shew unto his servants things which must shortly come to pass." Originally published as *Pearls of Wisdom,* they are of vital import to the servants of God throughout the earth.

The pouring out of the seven vials of the seven last plagues by the seven archangels who have come forth in the year of our Lord, nineteen hundred seventy-five, from out the Temple of the Tabernacle of the Testimony, marks the hour of the judgment when people of God everywhere are compelled to choose whether to walk to the right or to the left of the path of righteousness—the path of the right use of the laws governing God's energy. The vials of the seven last plagues are the judgments of Almighty God taken from the Book of Life and delivered to his people by the angelic hosts for the salvation of their souls through repentance, redemption, and regeneration in the Word.

In these teachings is the coming of the promised Comforter whom Jesus said the Father would send to teach us all things and to bring to our remembrance all things that he taught us. In these teachings is that Spirit of Truth, the Holy Ghost whom Jesus said would testify of him. The teachings of the archangels and the archeiai are the light shining in the darkness of the centuries in an hour and a moment of earth's history that may very well precede the dawn of a golden age in Aquarius, if the people of earth will take the prophecies and the revelations of the Lord and use them to meet the urgent demands of personal and planetary crisis.

Charged with the light of the cosmic consciousness of the emissaries of God, these messages contain the necessary keys for individuals, families, communities, and nations to live the life that is God in the final quarter of the twentieth century. The seven archangels come to teach us how to deal with the energies of the judgment and how we can invoke the sacred fire to balance every jot and tittle of the law of our being. They teach us how to stand, face, and conquer our karma—the cause-effect sequences of God's energy which by free will we have set in motion in this and past lives.

These heavenly ministrants show us the meaning of the seven rays of God, their correct and incorrect use, and how these rays when mastered can be released through the threefold flame—heart, head, and hand—for the Christ victory of all. They point out mankind's misuses of the seven rays and they explain that the vials of the seven last plagues contain the misqualified energies of the people of earth which, through invocation to the Holy Spirit, to the Presence of the I AM THAT I AM, and to the Christ Self, can now be requalified with the consciousness of God.

This process of spiritual/material transmutation is referred to by Paul as "the washing of the water by the Word." It is the very alchemy of forgiveness that demands of mankind obedience to the laws governing both the science of the soul and the science of Matter, of which the Lord spoke to Isaiah: "Come now, and let us reason together, saith the LORD: though your sins be as scarlet, they shall be as white as snow; though they be red like crimson, they shall be as wool. If ye be willing and obedient, ye shall eat the good of the land: But if ye refuse and rebel, ye shall be devoured with the sword: for the mouth of the LORD hath spoken it."

The admonishments of the archangels are directed to all who recognize the laws of the cosmos and the energies of life as the reality of God in manifestation, to all who would return to the moving stream of life that is the consciousness of the Elohim and who are willing to walk the path of initiation all the way back to the Great Central Sun.

"Blessed is he that readeth, and they that hear the words of this prophecy, and keep those things which are written therein: for the time is at hand."

Contents

"Behold, I will send my messenger . . ."

In order that she might fulfill the high calling of the messenger of the ascended masters—the same God-free beings who delivered the word of the Lord to the prophets and teachers of Israel and to the avatars of East and West—Elizabeth Clare Prophet was initiated by Saint Germain, the hierarch of the Aquarian age, and by El Morya, Chief of the Darjeeling Council of the Great White Brotherhood. Together with her late husband, the messenger Mark L. Prophet, who founded The Summit Lighthouse in Washington, D.C., in 1958, Elizabeth Clare Prophet was called to set forth the teachings of the Great White Brotherhood for the next two-thousand-year cycle.

These teachings have been released as the Everlasting Gospel in Book I of *Climb the Highest Mountain,* which contains practical and scientific explanations of the mysteries of the Self and the soul's mastery of the energies of the cosmos, and in *Pearls of Wisdom,* weekly letters from the ascended masters to their chelas, Keepers of the Flame Lessons, and the numerous books and tapes published by The Summit Lighthouse for Church Universal and Triumphant during the eighteen years of the Prophets' ministry.

Responding to the call of the Holy Spirit to bring the testimony of the Logos to the people, the messengers have held conferences and seminars throughout the United States and abroad. In 1971 they founded Summit University to offer disciples of East and West the ongoing revelations of the Christ and the Buddha and techniques for self-mastery and self-realization through the I AM Presence. Seeing the great need for children of all ages to prepare for the Path that leads to the one Source, they also founded Montessori International, a private school (preschool through the twelfth grade) to provide the foundations of excellence in secular education as well as a true culture of the soul.

On February 26, 1973, Mark Prophet took his leave of this earth, ascending to the plane of the I AM Presence to carry on his work with the ascended masters and to make contact with their unascended chelas yet striving toward the goal of reunion with the Source. And so the messengers, "the other two, the one on this side of the bank of the river and the other on that side of the bank of the river," remain the servants of the Lord and of his children in Spirit and in Matter "for a time, times and a half," as Daniel wrote, that "many shall be purified and made white, and tried" and that "the wise shall understand."

Elizabeth Clare Prophet, known today to the devotees of the teachings of the ascended masters as "Mother" because of her devotion to the flame of God as Mother, instructs and initiates students of cosmic law during twelve-week retreats sponsored by Jesus the Christ and Gautama the Buddha at Summit University. She also lectures and holds retreats throughout the world while continuing the important work of recording the teachings of the Great White Brotherhood and directing the multifaceted activities of Church Universal and Triumphant. The sacred responsibility of her mission, centered in the flame of God's will, is to teach, initiate, and succor the children of the Father-Mother God during this period of transition into the Aquarian age.

Another Sign in Heaven

And I saw another sign in heaven, great and marvellous, seven angels having the seven last plagues; for in them is filled up the wrath of God.

And I saw as it were a sea of glass mingled with fire: and them that had gotten the victory over the beast, and over his image, and over his mark, and over the number of his name, stand on the sea of glass, having the harps of God.

And they sing the song of Moses the servant of God, and the song of the Lamb, saying, Great and marvellous are thy works, Lord God Almighty; just and true are thy ways, thou King of saints.

Who shall not fear thee, O Lord, and glorify thy name? for thou only art holy: for all nations shall come and worship before thee; for thy judgments are made manifest.

And after that I looked, and, behold, the temple of the tabernacle of the testimony in heaven was opened:

And the seven angels came out of the temple, having the seven plagues, clothed in pure and white linen, and having their breasts girded with golden girdles.

And one of the four beasts gave unto the seven angels seven golden vials full of the wrath of God, who liveth for ever and ever.

And the temple was filled with smoke from the glory of God, and from his power; and no man was able to enter into the temple, till the seven plagues of the seven angels were fulfilled.

Revelation 15

A Great Voice Out of the Temple

And I heard a great voice out of the temple saying to the seven angels, Go your ways, and pour out the vials of the wrath of God upon the earth.

And the first went, and poured out his vial upon the earth; and there fell a noisome and grievous sore upon the men which had the mark of the beast, and upon them which worshipped his image.

And the second angel poured out his vial upon the sea; and it became as the blood of a dead man: and every living soul died in the sea.

And the third angel poured out his vial upon the rivers and fountains of waters; and they became blood.

And I heard the angel of the waters say, Thou art righteous, O Lord, which art, and wast, and shalt be, because thou hast judged thus.

For they have shed the blood of saints and prophets, and thou hast given them blood to drink; for they are worthy.

And I heard another out of the altar say, Even so, Lord God Almighty, true and righteous are thy judgments.

And the fourth angel poured out his vial upon the sun; and power was given unto him to scorch men with fire.

And men were scorched with great heat, and blasphemed the name of God, which hath power over these plagues: and they repented not to give him glory.

And the fifth angel poured out his vial upon the seat of the beast; and his kingdom was full of darkness; and they gnawed their tongues for pain,

And blasphemed the God of heaven because of their pains and their sores, and repented not of their deeds.

And the sixth angel poured out his vial upon the great river Euphrates; and the water thereof was dried up, that the way of the kings of the east might be prepared.

And I saw three unclean spirits like frogs come out of the mouth of the dragon, and out of the mouth of the beast, and out of the mouth of the false prophet.

For they are the spirits of devils, working miracles, which go forth unto the kings of the earth and of the whole world, to gather them to the battle of that great day of God Almighty.

Behold, I come as a thief. Blessed is he that watcheth, and keepeth his garments, lest he walk naked, and they see his shame.

And he gathered them together into a place called in the Hebrew tongue Armageddon.

And the seventh angel poured out his vial into the air; and there came a great voice out of the temple of heaven, from the throne, saying, It is done.

And there were voices, and thunders, and lightnings; and there was a great earthquake, such as was not since men were upon the earth, so mighty an earthquake, and so great.

And the great city was divided into three parts, and the cities of the nations fell: and great Babylon came in remembrance before God, to give unto her the cup of the wine of the fierceness of his wrath.

And every island fled away, and the mountains were not found.

And there fell upon men a great hail out of heaven, every stone about the weight of a talent: and men blasphemed God because of the plague of the hail; for the plague thereof was exceeding great.

Revelation 16

Michael, the Great Prince Which Standeth for the Children of Thy People

And at that time shall Michael stand up, the great prince which standeth for the children of thy people: and there shall be a time of trouble, such as never was since there was a nation even to that same time: and at that time thy people shall be delivered, every one that shall be found written in the book.

And many of them that sleep in the dust of the earth shall awake, some to everlasting life, and some to shame and everlasting contempt.

And they that be wise shall shine as the brightness of the firmament; and they that turn many to righteousness as the stars for ever and ever.

Daniel

THE FIRST VIAL

I

THE JUDGMENT OF THE FALLEN ONES

The First Vial

Children of the One:

I come by the authority of Alpha, in whose flaming presence I stand, before whose throne I bow. I am Michael, Archangel of the First Ray, anointed by Almighty God to minister unto the lifewaves in these several systems of worlds, commissioned in the holy of holies to defend the faith, the hope, the charity as the threefold flame of life which the Lord God has placed on the altar of the heart of every son and daughter that he has made.

I come in the flaming purity of the Christed ones. I come as the spokesman not only of the seven archangels, but also of the Lords of Karma and the seven chohans of the rays. For I come to fulfill the cosmic edict of the Lord "Behold, now is the accepted time: behold, now is the day of salvation."[1] This day of days is the acceptable day of the Lord's judgment. And indeed judgment is meted out from the judgment seat.

The seven archangels come forth bearing the vials of the seven last plagues. Robed in linen pure and white and girded with golden girdles, the seven archangels come forth from the Temple of the Tabernacle bearing the golden vials that are filled with the wrath of God.[2]

Well may it be said that the wrath of God is the wrath of man which the Lord God himself does turn against the idolatrous generation. And unto the seven archangels is given the task of delivering the coils of mankind's karma not alone on this planet or this system of worlds, but on planets in numberless systems where the fruit of the tree of the knowledge of good and evil has been partaken of by the man and the woman whom the Lord God hath made.[3]

Now behold how the Lords of Karma and the Four and Twenty Elders[4] stand back with heads bowed as the seven plagues of mankind's misuse of the sacred fire are turned upon them by the Lord God of hosts, by the law that is infallible and irrevocable—the same law that does govern the cycles of a cosmos and the inbreath and the outbreath of the seven Spirits of the seven Elohim,[5] the same law that governs the harmony of the spheres and the rolling chords of cosmic consciousness. This is the law which declares unto man ascended and man unascended, "Till heaven and earth pass, one jot or one tittle shall in no wise pass from the law, till all be fulfilled."[6]

Now we make contact with the light-bearers who are one in the Christ consciousness, one in the threefold flame of love, wisdom, and power. You who form the chain of hierarchy among the evolutions of God unascended, behold now the seven archangels, their white robes distinguished by the sashes of the seven rays—my own a brilliant sapphire blue focusing the protection and the perfection of the will of God on the first ray.

Behold Jophiel of the second ray with the golden yellow of the Cosmic Christ, the wisdom of the law perfecting the Logos in the minds of the children of God, and Chamuel wearing the rose pink, the love of the Holy Spirit that is for the fusion of twin flames on the third ray and the release of the creativity of God among the nations.

Gabriel, in the sash of the seraphim, represents the white of purity and the discipline of the fourth ray required for those desiring the reunion with God in the ascension through the dedication of the Mother flame; and Raphael stands with the emerald green focusing the truth of the fifth ray that is the liberation of the children of God from the error of the fallen ones—the truth that brings healing in its wings and the science of the Mother.

Uriel the Archangel, bearing the purple and gold of the Lord Christ, ministers unto his flocks in the ritual of the sixth ray of service, imparting the essence of the body and blood of Christ; and Archangel Zadkiel, in the ritual of the seventh ray, honors the violet fire of freedom in the name of Saint Germain for the liberation of every soul through the alchemy of forgiveness in the Aquarian age.

We come with our legions and with the archeiai in attendance. We come as the temple is filled with smoke from the glory of God and from his power;[7] and the smoke is the rising of the energies of the Holy Spirit that are now come upon mankind for the judgment. Rejoice, children of the One! Children of the light, rejoice! For, lo, with the coming of the judgment is the realization of your own fiery destiny!

Judgment is the alignment of energies to the right and to the left of the flame. Judgment is the all-seeing eye focusing right and wrong to the consciousness and to souls of light and souls of darkness. Judgment is the opportunity to see every infraction of the law within and without. Judgment is the measuring of the measure of man and woman by the rod of the law and by the scepter of his authority.

Now comes the great voice out of the temple

speaking to the seven archangels, "Go your ways and pour out the vials of the wrath of God upon the earth."[8] In this hour of the Dark Cycle's turning when mankind reap the karma of their abuses of the feminine ray and of the energies of the white-fire core anchored in the base-of-the-spine chakra, the law does require the children of the light to pursue the transmutation of the misuse of these sacred energies in the seven rays that converge in the white flame of the Mother.[9]

And so, let mankind behold the white robes of the saints. Let them see the purity of dedication focused in the auras of those who have gotten the victory over the beast and over his image and over his mark and over the number of his name.[10] Let those who march with the Divine Mother carrying the banner of Maitreya, the Cosmic Christ, call forth the sacred fire from their own causal bodies of light, from the I AM THAT I AM,[11] to consume the cause and core of the disintegration and the death that is the record of the murder of the Divine Mother and the slaughter of the holy innocents that has been enacted again and again on Lemuria, on Atlantis, and in every civilization ancient and modern where the fallen ones have moved in with their darkness and their deviltry, their degradation of the image of the Woman and their degeneration of the energies of the children of the light.

Now comes the judgment of the fallen ones! And with the descent of the fires of judgment none are spared. All must give accounting this day, for this is the day of salvation. The beloved Alpha before whose presence we chant the "Holy, Holy, Holy"[12] announced the binding of the Fallen One which occurred according to the cycles of Terra on April 16, 1975.[13]

The invocations of the two witnesses[14] made simultaneously above and below in the octaves of Spirit and Matter for the binding of that Lucifer were fulfilled by the seven archangels and the hosts of the Lord Christ. And so the duty and the dharma fell to us to bind that one and to remand him to the Court of the Sacred Fire convoked on the God Star Sirius, where the Four and Twenty Elders tried and sentenced the archdeceiver of mankind to the second death.[15] "Now is come salvation and strength and the kingdom of our God and the power of his Christ: for the accuser of our brethren is cast down, which accused them before our God day and night."[16]

With the Fallen One, many who followed him in the Great Rebellion were also brought to trial. And these trials are continuing as day by day the end of the cycle of opportunity for repentance comes to those who for thousands of years have refused to bend the knee and bow before the Lord Christ and to acknowledge the supremacy of the flaming Word incarnate in the sons and daughters of God. Thus while judgment is passed by the Four and Twenty Elders, judgment comes also to those in incarnation on numbers of planets where the end of cycles is also come.

Therefore is judgment meted out; and I am come forth bearing the golden vial containing mankind's wrathful, most dreadful misuses of the sacred fire on the first ray of the will of God. And it shall come to pass ere the year is fulfilled that the vision of John the Revelator shall be known of mankind and there shall fall "a noisome and grievous sore upon the men which have the mark of the beast and upon them that worship his image."[17]

I say to the children of the One: In this hour of salvation, it is your duty and your dharma to challenge the carnal mind in the name of the Christ; and it is your privilege in the name of the living God to challenge the Antichrist and to call forth the legions of Victory to give mankind the flaming consciousness of victory over the beast and over his image and over his mark and over the number of his name. So let it be done in the name of the living God, and let it be fulfilled—heart, head, and hand—through the children of the light!

This day will the Lord God reenact the judgment of the fallen ones through you as you give voice in the power of the spoken Word to the fiats of the Lord. Take then the decrees and invocations vouchsafed to you by the two witnesses,[18] and let your voices be the rising of the smoke of incense that is pleasing unto the Lord.[19] And let your voices rise in invocation in affirmation of the judgment twenty-four hours a day.

From out the Temple of the Tabernacle of the Testimony I am come. And I come with deliverance to the nations and to the captives of the Luciferians; and I come to deliver the mandate of the Lord God—the mandate of mankind's own karma. Now let us see how the intensification of the sacred fire in the hearts of the devotees will be the all-consuming flame of the Holy Spirit that clears a pathway through the dark night of the soul over which the children of Israel may pass unto the light of the new day.

O children of Zion, come to the sun of the I AM THAT I AM and fall down in worship of the Lord Christ, lest ye be judged with the fallen ones and with the Antichrist! Therefore, let the nations and the generations of all peoples be converted this day to the kindling light of love, wisdom, and power that is the eternal Christos of your soul's own God-identity.

I am Michael, Prince of the Archangels. I stand on the side of the north of the City Foursquare,[20] and my right hand is raised to release the light of the Presence. In the words of Alpha I say, "Children of the One: Forge your God-identity!"

Michael

Archangel of the First Ray

II

THE JUDGMENT OF THE DWELLER ON THE THRESHOLD

The Vigil of Faith

Children of the One Who Would Join the Armies of the Faithful and True:

I am Faith, guardian of the flame of Michael the Archangel. I ensoul the Mother light of faith in the mission of my beloved. I stand with the women of the world and with the Woman clothed with the Sun,[1] the defender of the God consciousness.

I am that consciousness rising as the bow of faith from which the arrows of hope and charity are sent by the hand of the Eternal Archer to the hearts of the children of God everywhere. I hold the immaculate concept for your faith, and I keep the home fires burning while Michael and his legions go forth to do battle with the dragon and his fallen angels.[2]

Women of the world—you to whom is given in this moment of cosmic destiny the opportunity to keep the flame for the sons and daughters of God—come to me as I draw you close to my heart of living faith.

Faith is the power by which your dreams come true.
Faith is the will to be and to do.
Faith is the action of the sacred Word.

Faith is the voice of God I heard.
I see you as you are.
I know you as you were.
I supply the energy to confer
The immaculate conception of your origin in God.

Mothers of the world, it is your faith in your children, your husbands, and your loved ones that will see them through their night in Gethsemane, their hour before the tribunals of earth and heaven, their moment of surrender on the cross of Alpha and Omega, and the three cycles[3] in the tomb of Mater where they, too, must work out the problem of life and death, the problem of the planes of consciousness and their infiltration by the astral hordes.

It was the faith of an archeia that was focused in the vigil of the three Marys.[4] By faith they kept the vigil at the cross; by faith they stood at the door of the tomb; by faith they beheld the risen Saviour. You, too, must uphold your faith in the sons and daughters of God in the moment of supreme testing. With Aaron and Hur, you must hold up the hands of Moses for the great and notable day of the Lord's victory; and by faith you shall see the discomfiture of Amalek and his people with the edge of the sword of truth wielded by Joshua, the chosen one.[5] Let your faith be the soaring of consciousness that shall mount up with wings as eagles[6] bearing the hopes of mankind to the altar of God where in the flame of your living faith he will implement the plan divine.

I come on the wings of Archangel Michael to speak to you concerning the golden vial that he has released and the karma of its contents. Indeed this plague is a dark energy that covers the sky at noonday as though the hand of God had scattered the dust of the centuries, distributing to the four winds mankind's willful pollution of the elements of being.

In this hour of the judgment, the Lord God has not left you comfortless,[7] O my children. The sword of Kali is a comfort to all who adore the Mother flame. And to all who would be in the center of the fires of the Holy Spirit, the Comforter is come! And it is given unto you to stand on the sea of glass mingled with fire, to place your feet on the platform of Almighty God that he has lowered into manifestation for your refuge, for your strength, for your overcoming of all darkness by the sacred essence of the Lamb of God.

Therefore, sing the song of Moses![8] Sing the name of God, I AM THAT I AM! And chant the AUM into the night and into the day. It is your homing—your call to the Father-Mother God. And your callings are the weavings of your soul weaving the ladder of light, even Jacob's ladder[9] whereby the angels of our band, ascending and descending, provide the way of escape to all who worship the Christ, and him only, in the love of living and in the life of loving all free.

Therefore, sing the song of the Lamb, saying: "Great and marvellous are thy works, Lord God Almighty; just and true are thy ways, thou King of saints. Who shall not fear thee, O Lord, and glorify thy name? for thou only art holy: for all nations shall come and worship before thee; for thy judgments are made manifest."[10] And this shall be the mantra of those who espouse the flames of Michael and Faith for the victory of the Lord's hosts. This is the mantra that was given by the angel of Jesus Christ unto John the Revelator that you in this hour of the victory might have the sacred Word to implement the victory by the sword of the Spirit.[11]

Now my legions come forth! And they stand before the altar of the Divine Mother and before her representative on earth. They stand before the children of God to bind the powers of darkness, of doubt and fear, of the spirals of disintegration and death.

For in the flaming presence of faith is the transmutative action of the law. This is the hour for the reaping of the sowings of doubt and fear and death. Therefore the angels are come to take from you the harvest of your wrong sowings in the will of God. Prepare yourselves; and let them come to separate the tares and the wheat[12] of your consciousness, and let them gather the tares that they might be burned in the sacred fire of the will of God.

See them come; for they, too, are of the armies of the Faithful and True. The Faithful and True is the Lord Christ who comes to claim his own, and his armies roll in numberless array.[13] See them as they come marching from the Court of the Sacred Fire! And there is no end to the heavenly formation that descends this day with the great teams of conquerors to proclaim deliverance to those that have been brought captive before the unrighteous generation.

As you enter the fray, enjoining the hosts of the Lord, put on the whole armor of God that ye may be able to stand against the wiles of the lieutenants of Lucifer.[14] These are the devils who have *d*eified *evil,* who have worshiped the golden calf[15] and raised up the carnal mind to pervert the serpentine energies of the caduceus, which even Moses raised up in the wilderness as the sign of Christ's healing wholeness unto the children of Israel.[16]

Face squarely the enemy within and without and receive the admonishment of Alpha, who has declared:

> Now let all evolutions and lifewaves know: The challenge of the hour is the consuming by the sacred fire of the cause, effect, record, and memory of all that has been impressed upon the body of the Mother—that body the entire cosmos—by the fallen ones. Now let us behold how the Fallen One has left seeds of rebellion even in the four lower bodies

of the children of God. And so the Evil One came and sowed the tares among the wheat.

Now let the sons of light go forth! Let them go into the fields white with the harvest. Let them, as the reapers with the angelic hosts, separate the tares from the wheat. And let it be done by the fiat of Alpha and Omega! Let it be done by the action of the flow of sacred fire from the I AM Presence of each one!

More dangerous even than the Fallen One are the seeds of rebellion that remain to be consumed, for the seed contains within itself the pattern of the whole. And therefore I release the light of the fiery core of the flow of our oneness for the canceling-out of the seed of the Fallen One. I release this energy to the level of the etheric plane, the plane of fire. Farther it cannot go without the assent of your free will and your invocation, for the sacred fire will burn and consume the wheat with the tares unless it first be assimilated in the consciousness of the light-bearers.

Let the sacred fire, then, in the increment that can be borne by each one, be sealed in the third eye and the crown and in the heart as a trinity of action that can be called forth and released in the plane of the mind and the mental belt of a cosmos. It is the mind of Christ that the fallen ones have determined to seize, to misuse. They have no power from Alpha and Omega; yet the fiery core of life within the children of the sun has been used to affirm that power, to acquiesce to it and to reinforce it.

I say then, withdraw by the authority of your free will all affirmation, all consent that you have given unto the fallen ones, unto their rebellion, unto the seed, and unto the carnal mind of your own creation. Only thus will the mental belt be cleansed of the remnant of the Fallen One.

Now let the beast that occupies the bottomless pit of the subconscious and the desire body be exposed also! And let it be seen that this creation instigated by the fallen ones has also received the seal of your approval. For that which remains untransmuted, which you have failed to challenge, that which exists in consciousness, is therefore the creation of free will. And until you will to call it back, to undo it, to restore it to the fiery core for transmutation, it remains a blight on the whole of cosmos.

Only when you challenge the dweller on the threshold of your own cosmos and your own consciousness—the rebellious one—can you breathe the breath of life and know "I AM free!" Therefore, that judgment that has come to the Fallen One, meted out by Alpha and Omega, must also resound within the consciousness of every living soul. And the Alpha-to-Omega, the atom of identity in the fiery core of your own being, must release the spiral that renders the judgment whereby the dweller on the threshold passes through the second death and is no more and has no longer any habitation in the whole consciousness of that life which you call your own, but which I am here to tell you is my very own—mine to give, mine to take. And I can claim that fiery core, that replica of the Great Central Sun, when the cycles roll and the law of being returns the drop unto the Ocean.

> You have a cosmos! You have an energy field assigned to you! Let the four quadrants of your creation be purged of every residue of the Fallen One! Let them be purged by your free will aligned with my own, aligned with the Four and Twenty Elders who render judgment in the God Star. And let the earth body as well be free of the impressions of rebellion and the ego that is set apart from the Divine One![17]

And so, my beloved children, by faith let us forge our God-identity. Let us hearken unto the message of Alpha and know that as we fulfill the word of the Father-Mother God, we shall be the Word incarnate. As above, so below, we are the oneness of the divine union. And our son, Micah, Angel of Unity, encircles the earth, traversing the lines of longitude. He with his angels of unity carry the flaming sword to slay the dragons roaming the continents of the mind to divide and conquer the body of God upon earth.

For faith, for unity in the will of God,

I AM

Faith

Archeia of the First Ray

THE SECOND VIAL

III

THE JUDGMENT OF MANKIND'S PERVERSION OF THE WISDOM OF THE MOTHER

The Second Vial

Children of the One
Pursuing the Way of Illumined Action:

I am the archangel of the dawn of illumination. I clear the way for illumined action and for the light of understanding. By my flame the author of Proverbs wrote: "Wisdom is the principal thing; therefore get wisdom: and with all thy getting get understanding. Exalt her, and she shall promote thee: she shall bring thee to honour when thou dost embrace her. She shall give to thine head an ornament of grace: a crown of glory shall she deliver to thee."[1]

So is the raising-up of the rod of wisdom's power the action of the second ray. And the angels of illumination do minister to mankind in this hour of judgment, that they might raise up the energies of the Divine Mother as she is known among us by the name of Wisdom. Therefore doth Wisdom teach her children the raising of the energies of the sacred fire to form the crown of glory that is the halo, the hallowed life-force, of the crown of the Buddha, the crown of the Christ, the crown of the kings and queens.

Sons and daughters of God born to rule by the

rod of understanding, let the understanding of the Christ confute the philosophy and the psychicism of the fallen ones! Let the illumined action of the light-bearers show forth the light of salvation! Let the action of those who work the works of God with compassionate understanding be the great example by which the teachings of the Great White Brotherhood are made clear—clear as the sea of glass mingled with fire.

And the golden vial of the second angel is poured upon the sea, and the emotional bodies of mankind are agitated as the astral plane becomes as the blood of a dead man, and the souls of the living cannot survive in the sea of the astral plane.[2] We walk through the valley of the shadow of death.[3] We walk through the canyons of the astral; and our light, as the brilliance of the noonday sun, as the light of the causal bodies of the heavenly hosts, does expose the remnant of the Liar and his lie.[4]

And they recoil in the presence of the archangels. Where have they to go? None can escape the Lord God in the hour of judgment. "Therefore for judgment I am come," saith the Lord. And their recoiling is the driving-back of the energies of the fallen ones. And they are driven back into the white-fire core wherein the error of their wrong choosing is become the consuming of the white-fire yellow-fire sun.

And the consuming of the pollution of the waters of the living Word is the consummation of the Mother and the Holy Spirit. The understanding of the Mother is the wellspring of life[5] unto all who have retained the law of the Father. Let the wellspring of the Mother rising from the base-of-the-spine chakra be the focus of purity's transmutation of all misunderstanding. For misunderstanding is the mist that went up from the earth as the maya, the veil of evil that watered the whole face of the ground.[6]

Now is the vial of mankind's misuse of the Mother

flow poured out upon the sea. And those who dwell in the sea must forge here and now that God-identity which is a fire infolding itself[7]—that God-identity that is able by the flame upon the altar of the heart to consume all mankind's misuses of the sacred fire perverting the wisdom of the Divine Mother in the second ray of illumined action.

Yes, I am Jophiel. I consecrate places of learning where souls are yearning to be free through the mastery of the mind of God. Unfortunately, the fallen ones have usurped the seat of authority; and they sit in the philosopher's chair instructing the children of the light in the ways of darkness. And discrimination is nowhere to be found, save in the teachings of the Mother.

I come wielding the sword of discrimination that by the flame of wisdom you might join my bands as they thrust home to the core of the luciferian creation to cleave asunder the real from the unreal, that the motives and intents of the heart of a planet and a people might be laid bare in this hour of the tenth station of the cross when those who take their stand for the Lord incarnate are stripped of their garments by the Roman soldiers.[8] I say, let the fallen ones also submit to the stations of the cross! Let them be stripped of their temporal power and of their authority in the governments of the nations!

Let those who have led the children of God into captivity now go into the captivity of the Holy Spirit. And let the cloven tongues of fire[9] strip from them their carnality and their sensuality which they have put upon the children of God as a smothering cloak of unrighteousness. And let him that killeth with the sword be killed with the sword.[10] This is the sword of the sacred Word of wisdom; this is the sword that consumes all that is unreal.

Therefore those who identify with unreality shall

be no more in that day of the judgment of the Lord. And let the patience and the faith of the saints[11] keep the flame of life and light and illumination as darkness covers the land and the sea and the only light that shines is the light of the I AM Presence.

Let the warning be sounded forth by the angels of Jophiel's band that all those who have taken the word of God and the true teachings of the law and perverted the divine credo of the Holy Spirit shall face the judgment of the Almighty. And let the false prophets and the wolves in sheep's clothing[12] who have usurped the pulpits of the world be stripped of their garments! And let them stand naked before the children of God, who will then see the wickedness of their ways and the evil machinations which they have put upon this generation.

Let the clarity of the mind of Christ flow! Let golden rivers of illumination flow from the throne of God! Let rivers of light inundate consciousness and clear the way for the true teachings of the law! I stand upon the earth this hour and I stand upon the sea, and I make way for the coming of the Lord and of the law of life. And I clear the consciousness of mankind that they might receive wisdom at the hand of the Mother.

In this hour of reckoning comes the angel of opportunity sent forth by Portia, the Goddess of Justice. This angel is the mercy of the law and of the karma of the seven last plagues. And opportunity is a scroll declaring the independence of the souls of Terra ratified by the saints above and below. This declaration is the open door for the wisdom teachings.

Let the holy Kumaras release the light of the seven rays in the minds of mankind. And let the quickening that was begun at Shasta by the Elohim of the Second Ray[13] be intensified even as darkness is intensified before the dawn of the Christ consciousness in mankind. This is that increment of light which is delivered once in ten thousand years by the holy Kumaras. It is a rod implanted in the minds of the children of God by the Solar Logoi for the elevation of mankind's consciousness and the centering of that consciousness in the crown. So intensify! So magnify! So let the star be brilliant in its appearing and let mankind be polarized to that star of the light of wisdom!

Let the wise man and woman entering the Aquarian cycle hear the word of wisdom's ray and increase learning and attain unto the wise counsels of the Four and Twenty Elders. Now let the fear of the Lord come upon mankind—that fear that is the beginning of knowledge.[14] For this is the age of opportunity, the age when the Lord giveth wisdom. And out of the mouth of his messengers cometh knowledge and understanding. This is the Lord who keepeth the paths of judgment and preserveth the way of his saints.

Let illumination's fires be invoked for the consuming of all false doctrine and dogma, all misstatements and misunderstandings of the law. Let Wisdom crystallize the image of the Christ within you.

Yes, I am come with the golden vial of the second of the last plagues. But I come also with opportunity at my side. Let the children of the light run into the wave of wisdom's light. Let them run into the great cosmic wave of illumination that breaks upon the shores of Mater and floods the consciousness with the refreshing waters purified by the Mother of life and love and liberation.

Run to greet the wave of light and see how the great wave will swallow up the pollutions of the river of life.[15] I am for oneness only if it be the oneness of the Christ mind. And those who defy that mind in my servants the prophets shall be scattered abroad; for they are the proud, the rebellious, and the unrighteous generation.

I am at the door. Bidden by the Lord, I enter.

And I come to overthrow the moneychangers in the temple of our God.[16] I come to scourge the wicked generation. See then that you, the light-bearers, are allied with the light, lest when the judgment come it scorch the wings of an angel!

I AM

Jophiel

of the Flame

IV

RATIFY AND CONFIRM THE JUDGMENT WITHIN YOUR OWN BEING

The Opening of the Door of Consciousness

Children of the One Who Would Bear the Torch of Illumination to an Age:

I am the eternal light of the Christos in the feminine ray. I am the Archeia of the Second Ray. I come in the flaming consciousness of the Christ, of the King of Kings and Lord of Lords;[1] for I am the champion of the Christed ones.

Sons and daughters of God who walk the earth in the light of the Logos unmoved by human tyranny or the condemnation of the fallen ones, you who keep the flame of life, know that I am with you in the intelling Presence of the I AM THAT I AM and that I send angels of Jophiel and Christine who come in the name of the Cosmic Virgin to protect the consciousness of all who love the Lord with all their hearts and souls and minds.[2]

Wherever there is a glimmer of the light of the Christ, wherever there is a flickering in the consciousness and then a bursting-forth of a facet of the mind of God, there the angels of illumination are magnetized to enhance that energy, to enlighten minds and hearts and souls already one in the mission of the Lord and Saviour.

To acknowledge him is to open the door to your own Christ-identity, and to deny him is to close that door. And this is the message of the Spirit of the Christ unto the churches: "Behold, I stand at the door and knock: if any man hear my voice and open the door, I will come in to him and will sup with him, and he with me."[3]

The opening of the door of consciousness is a sacred ritual that must be performed by the children of God in this age. To open the door to the Christ and to the seven Spirits of God [the seven Elohim] and to the seven stars [the seven causal bodies of the seven rays][4] is to open the heart and the chakra of the heart to the love-wisdom-power of the Logos. When you consciously, willingly allow the Christos to enter there, the divine spark is quickened by emissaries of the heavenly hierarchy who have already attained to the measure of a God flame and its manifestation.

Understand, then, that to reject the heavenly hosts and the Faithful and True who leads the armies of heaven into the battle of Armageddon[5] is to seal the door of consciousness against the light of your own Christ-perfection. And this is the dread of the seven archangels—that when we enter the octaves of earth we find no room in the inn of being, no chamber in the heart where we are welcome, and the light of the Mother is rejected by those who fear her all-consuming love.

The Lord God has said, "Seal the door where evil dwells!" But mankind have inverted the command and sealed the door of the Christ consciousness to their own hurt and their own destruction. The dread of the archangels is the dread of the awful day of judgment—awful only for those who have sealed themselves from the contact of the Christed ones and the blessed tie of hierarchy that binds mankind to the law of his own inner being.

Hear then the words of Jesus the Christed One to the inhabiters of the Holy City: "O Jerusalem, Jerusalem, thou that killest the prophets and stonest them which are sent unto thee, how often would I have gathered thy children together, even as a hen gathereth her chickens under her wings, and ye would not! Behold, your house is left unto you desolate. For I say unto you, Ye shall not see me henceforth, till ye shall say, Blessed is he that cometh in the name of the Lord."[6]

See how the pure person of the Christ extending through flesh and blood the love of God and of the great brooding presence of the Cosmic Virgin, symbolized in the hen that gathereth her chickens under her wings, was not able to turn the hardness of their hearts that to this day is the rejection of the Christ consciousness on Terra. And therefore in every century the children of God and the children of the wicked one have the opportunity to stand in the presence of the one who is anointed for that cycle to be the Word incarnate.

And to all who reject the person of the Christ in the sons and daughters of God, the edict of the Lord is delivered: "Ye shall not see me henceforth, till ye shall say, Blessed is he that cometh in the name of the Lord." To receive the Christed ones in the name of Jesus the Christ is to seal your own Christ-identity. And when you ratify the presence of the threefold flame within you, lo, you behold standing before you the risen Saviour!

My name is Christine because I have enshrined the light of the *Christ in* the *e*nergies of Mater. I ensoul the eternal Christos in the fiery core of the atom as my service to the Cosmic Virgin. I keep the flame of cosmic intelligence as the intelling love of God, as the indwelling wisdom, as God telling the ancient story of the Word and of the law and of the power of his name in the hearts of all the creation—in elemental life, in the plants and the trees and the gentle creatures. For although they have not the Christ-intelligence of the threefold flame, they have that inner intuition of the intelling of the Lord God.

Energy is God. And therefore the core of energy, as that energy flows from Spirit to Matter and returns again, is the Mediator, the Christed One, the great transformer of the energies of life. In the white-fire core of the atom is the point for the transition of consciousness as above, so below. Energy is God—self-luminous, intelligent, obedient to the law of the One. Wherever there is intelligence, there I AM amplifying the flow of the intelligent electron. More intelligent than the rebellious generation who have usurped the light of God's energy are these electrons who have elected to do and to be the will of God. Their flow is with the flow of the eternal Christos.

You see, God's energy will not forever be confined to the limitations and the imitations of the counterfeit creation. As the Lord has said, "My Spirit shall not always strive with man, for that he also is flesh."[7] The Lord God will not forever allow himself as energy to be imprisoned in the matrices of imperfection.

Therefore cometh the judgment. Therefore the second angel, my own beloved Jophiel, has poured out his vial upon the sea. Let all who worship God release the golden light of illumination's fires that the sea might be glazed with the golden light of the sun and that that sun might form the pathway over which the sons and daughters of God walk in witness of the truth.

I am the consciousness of Wisdom that teacheth her children. I am in the heart of every mother that rocks the infant Messiah, imparting the flow of knowledge and understanding. And now I quote for your benefit the words of Alpha, who counseled the children of the light to confirm the judgment within their own being:

Let all be alert! Let all know that the passing from the Macrocosm of the one who instigated the rebellion of the angels is a point for the release of great light in the Macrocosm. You are globules of identity suspended in the Macrocosm of my own self-awareness. And that light which inundates the cosmic sea cannot penetrate the sphere of identity which you are unless you will it so. Therefore I come to say: Ratify and confirm the judgment within your own being; and only then be satisfied in the law and in the victory.

Judgment is nigh. Understand that unless you release the judgment in your own microcosm and withdraw all support of the energy veil, when the judgment comes and the skeins of consciousness are found to be woven inextricably with skeins of evil, then the entire globule must pass through the spirals of Alpha and Omega. And this is the ritual, then, of the canceling-out of that which cannot be absorbed into the sea; for by free will it has not willed it so.

You are set apart as a diamond suspended in crystal, suspended in ruby, suspended in agate. See how the crystallization of the God flame which I am must be made your own. You determine the fate of your own cosmos. So let it be. So receive the warning that perhaps there is even greater danger now than when the Adversary was personified before you; for now it remains only the subjective awareness, and that subjectivity is the burden of the soul that longs to be extricated from that substance that has no part with light.

I AM Alpha. I AM Omega. When you know that you are Alpha, that you are Omega,

> then—and only then—will you find yourself in
> the white-fire core of the Great Central Sun.
> Children of the One: *Forge your God-identity!*[8]

Let the sun of God expand within your heart and let your meditations be upon the blessed sun—expanding, expanding as the brilliant golden white light from the altar of your very own heart. When you give your mantras and invocations, when you recite your decrees definitive of the divinity within you—above all, when you pray to our Father-Mother God—let not your attention be attenuated in outer manifestation, but rather let it be concentrated in the heart.

And as that heart fire expands and expands, taking in the all of your being and your four lower bodies, you will be confirming the judgment of the law. You will be refining your soul energies in the great cloud of the Spirit. You will be building the forcefield of the Great Central Sun magnet that will surely magnetize to you, even as I AM THAT I AM, the heavenly hosts who nourish and sustain the children of God through all of the trials and tribulations of this world.

Therefore intensify, O intensify that sun! See it now! Adore its golden glow! Feel the intensity of the love of the Logos within you contacting all throughout a cosmos and beyond who adore the one supreme God. By the power of the central sun focused within you, the Christ will put down the carnal mind, the Christ will consume the dweller on the threshold and all subconscious layers of selfishness and rebellion against the one true God. Your soul longs to be free. Take then the mantra of the free! Forge your God-identity with this saying of the Lord: "I AM Alpha and Omega in the white-fire core of being!"

Let this be the acceptable word of the Lord that comes forth from your mouth, the sacred instrument of the voice of God. Let this be the acceptable word, the fiat and the command uttered unto the atoms, molecules, and precious electrons of being. "I AM Alpha and Omega in the white-fire core of being!" Let this be your finding of yourself in the white-fire core of the central sun on this the acceptable day of salvation and the appointed time of the judgment.

Children of the One: Forge your God-identity!

I AM

Christine

of the light of the Christos

THE THIRD VIAL

V

THE JUDGMENT OF MANKIND'S PERVERSION OF THE FIRES OF CREATIVITY

The Third Vial

Children of the One Who Would Dwell
in the Flaming Presence of Love:

I am Chamuel, and I descend from spheres of love to decelerate the intensity of God's love that you might receive him. This is the tempering of the wind to the shorn lamb of mankind's identity. For the winds of the Holy Spirit and the fires infolded in the winds are indeed for the judgment of the luciferian creation and for the intensification of love in the hearts of the lightbearers, that love itself might be the instrument of the judgment.

Let your hearts now burn within you![1] For the Presence of the Lord, though unseen and unknown, is nigh. And you will recognize the reality of your Lord and your Saviour by the burning of your heart in the love of the Creator. For only the Saviour, the eternal Christos, who lives in the hearts of ascended and unascended beings, can cause the quickening of the fires on earthly altars—the same fires that burn as votive flames ignited by angels who keep the flame of life on behalf of souls moving in the planes of Mater.

Just as the quickening must come in the hearts of

the children of God on the notable day of the Lord, so the quaking must also come in the hearts of those who have rebelled against the light. It is their hearts that will fail them for fear[2] of the judgment which is come.

Therefore in answer to the edict of the Lord, I come forth from the Temple of the Tabernacle of the Testimony carrying the golden vial that contains mankind's wrathful misuses of the energies of love. What do you think, O mankind, will come upon this generation who have taken the very fires of creativity, the very energies of the Holy Spirit, and perverted them against the light of the One! I say, let judgment reign! And let it be the raining of the fires of the Almighty One as I pour out the measure of mankind's karma upon the rivers and fountains of waters for them to become blood.[3]

And now let the response of the angel of the waters be heard: "Thou art righteous, O Lord, which art and wast and shalt be, because thou hast judged thus. For they have shed the blood of saints and prophets, and thou hast given them blood to drink; for they are worthy."[4] And let the angel standing at the altar of the Most High God give the mantra of the third ray, "Even so, Lord God Almighty, true and righteous are thy judgments."[5] And let this mantra be heard by God from the lips of the righteous who have learned the right use of love and who have consecrated the energies of the Holy Spirit in the rituals of the sacred fire.

Of all of the misuses of the sacred fire which mankind have imposed upon nature and the body of the Mother, there is none more deadly or more dastardly than the perversion of divine love. Let the children of the light call forth the intense action of the violet flame from the master of the Aquarian age, Saint Germain, who focuses the consciousness of God-love in this system of worlds! For this is a generation of people-haters, children-haters, Christ-haters, and God-haters; and mankind's hearts have become hardened against the true children of Israel—the children of the light of all that is real.

And as Pharaoh hardened his heart to the word of the Lord that came through Moses and to the judgments of the Lord that turned the waters to blood and brought pestilence, affliction, and the death of the firstborn in the houses of the Egyptians,[6] so are the hearts of mankind hardened to the word of the Lord delivered unto this age through the two witnesses. And they and their children and the true followers of God are hated—despised and rejected of men.[7] And thus it has been through all of the centuries when the sons and daughters of God have come to deliver the sheep of the Good Shepherd from the toils of the Luciferians.

Through the pride of the eye and the degradation of the flame of the Mother, mankind have rejected their deliverers. They have imitated the ways of the fallen ones and scourged and spat upon the true Lamb of God. Like the dog that bites the hand that feeds it, mankind have been utterly duped to the place where, in their depressed state of consciousness, they follow the Pied Piper into the night and reject the marriage supper of the Lamb and the Lamb's wife.[8]

Now this is the dilemma of the archangels and of the Lords of Karma and of Alpha and Omega. As it has ever been, the light shone in the darkness and the darkness comprehended it not.[9] Therefore is judgment come, that mankind might learn from the taskmaster of their own karma that which is acceptable in the presence of love.

Let honor, longsuffering, and tenderness characterize the relationships of the followers of God. Let doctrine and dogma be consumed in the fires of love. Let the Holy Spirit unite all hearts in the love of the One. And let those who stand with Michael the

Archangel and all the archangels and their legions of light to defend the faith, the hope, and the charity of all mankind determine to put down, once and for all, the aggressive voices of the night that hammer the brain with their lies!

If you would get the victory over the beast and over his image and over his mark and over the number of his name, stand on the sea of glass! Stand on the purity of the Mother and her immaculate concept which she holds undefiled for each child of God. Put down the luciferian lie directed as an arrow of division into your mental body! Refute the lie concerning the Woman and her seed. Refute the lie concerning the Keepers of the Flame. Put down these demons of the night! For they come as the hordes of shadow to take over the consciousness of the children by rays of insanity and profanity, of psychicism, spiritism, hypnotism, and mental manipulation.

Aggressive mental suggestion is the germ warfare of the fallen ones. You must hold up the shield of the archangels and wield the sword of the Spirit to deflect the arrows of their outrageous consciousness. And they are raging in the stalls of the astral, like the Devil, that roaring lion, seeking whom they may devour.[10]

The fallen ones are organized. They have taken the consciousness of love, which is the very order of a cosmos, and perverted it to their own use. They have organized a warfare of the Spirit, projecting their vials of astral microbes, astral viruses, deadly toxins which they would inject into the mental and emotional bodies of mankind through that which we have called aggressive mental suggestion.

You can identify this energy. You can know it well. For at any moment of the day or night when you feel waves of irritation and mild dislike and a separation from brothers and sisters on the Path through barbs of criticism and waves of anxiety and nervous tension and you feel your energies seized with a certain dislike for this or that individual or an action of intense condemnation or judgment of a coservant who works side by side with you in the field of the Lord, know that the Devil has sent his angels, even Satan who has deceived the whole world.[11]

And though he be bound for a thousand years by Michael the Archangel of the Lord, who "cast him into the bottomless pit and shut him up and set a seal upon him, that he should deceive the nations no more,"[12] his angels enter into combat with the sons and daughters of God. This is Armageddon. This is the warfare of the Spirit "against principalities, against powers, against the rulers of the darkness of this world, against spiritual wickedness in high places."[13] You must be alert; for where there is gossip and where there is the maligning of the image of the Mother or her children, where there is the tearing-down of the activities of those who are serving—no matter how imperfectly—the cause of the Brotherhood, know that there are the fallen ones lurking in your midst to destroy the works of God on earth.

Hearken not to their counsel! Hearken to the Lord. Do not respond to their turbulence, their riptides of emotional energy which they unleash at the feet of the children of the light! Do you not know, O blessed ones, how they gather the clouds of darkness and the grids and forcefields of mankind's hatred and concentrate the misqualified energies of an entire city or a nation against one soul who is taking his stand for the light of truth?

If you would live in the flaming presence of love, be prepared to deal with the fallen ones who have misused this sacred fire to create all manner of ugliness and distortion of the divine arts and of the music of the spheres to turn man and woman upside down and inside out in acts of perverted sex and misuses of the sacred fire. And they have caused the judgment of Sodom and Gomorrah[14] to be upon this generation who have replaced reverence for life with the murder of the avatars and of the Divine Mother.

I am come for the judgment, that the energies of the Holy Spirit might be realigned in man and woman, that the fires of the kundalini might rise on the altar of the spine to illumine, to purify, and to increase the intensity of the sun behind the sun. Let mankind know, then, that their expulsion from Eden[15] came about as the result of their misuse of the sacred fire in oral sex, in cohabitation with animal life, in homosexuality and all manner of experimentation with the seed and the egg, including their creation of human and animal life in the test tubes of the laboratories of the laggard generation.

These things are the abomination of desolation standing in the holy place of the sacred union where they ought not.[16] Therefore judgment is come, and those that take the sword to kill the holy innocents while they are yet in their mothers' wombs must also be killed with the sword. For this day they are expelled from the womb of the Divine Mother! And this is the law and the judgment.

I shall take my leave of you, for even the children of the light have all that they can bear in the intensity of my message. There is weeping and gnashing of teeth[17] outside the womb of the Cosmic Virgin! Let those who would retain the right and the light to live in the flame of the Mother cease their desecration of her love.

I AM

Chamuel

standing on the south side of the City Foursquare

VI

THE FIRE OF LOVE DESCENDING TO IMPLEMENT THE JUDGMENT

Choose the Hallowed Circle of the Father-Mother God

Children of the One Who Would Learn to Love
and to Love and to Love:

I am Charity of the light, adornment of the sacred union of the Father-Mother God. I come to deliver mankind from the toils of selfish love. I come to deliver man and woman from the agony of self-centered love and of that which seeks to possess and is thereby possessed of the not-self.

See how the discarnates penetrate that which ought to be the hallowed circle of the love of the Father-Mother God sealed in the union of every son and daughter who have come before the altar of the Most High to consecrate their marriage vows! See how the envious ones lurk to steal the energies of the sacred fire that belong to you and to you alone!

I stand on the threshold of the circle of the oneness of twin flames. I am Charity, and I come to draw the hallowed circle of your union. I come as the patroness of the Holy Family in the Aquarian age. I come in the service of Saint Germain and Mary and the Lord Christ. For I have been bidden to come forth from the Temple of the Tabernacle of the Testimony of the Logos to protect the love of devotees serving in the planes of Mater.

O my children, the demons of the night are jealous of your love. They would claw the very body of the Mother if they could. They come as vultures to devour the flesh and blood of the children of God before the hour of the consecration of the body and the blood by the Sacred Eucharist of our Lord. They are not the eagles who gather together at the place of the corpus Christi.[1] They are not the sons and daughters of God who follow the flame of the Mother enshrined in the tower of the lighthouse—a beacon to guide the souls to victory—but they are the discarnates sent by the dragon to devour the child as soon as it is born.[2]

Cradle the child of your love. Wrap the child in the swaddling garments of the Holy Spirit. Let honor and reverence for one another be the pivot of a cosmic love unfolding in Mater to the glory of the eternal Christos. Remember the story of Sleeping Beauty. Each time the innocence of love is veiled in flesh, each time the Mother flame is born anew in Mater preparing to unite with the knight champion of the Holy Spirit, there appears on the scene, lurking in the shadows, the representative of the great whore[3] who comes to poison that rosy-cheeked innocence.

O my children, let your love be the commemoration of the fusion of the cloven tongues of the Spirit. Now then, take the ritual which the archangels practice at the rising and the setting of the sun when the torch of love is passed by angels of the dawn and angels of the dusk. Take the ritual of the archangels and make it all your own, and prove thereby the victory of love on Terra. Prove that your love is the holy habitation of the Lord God of hosts and that this love, by your will firmed in the fire of God-determination, will not be defiled by the hordes of the night.

Stand together facing the chart of the I AM

Presence (see illustration facing page 64) and make your inner attunement with the star of your divinity. Meditate upon your heart and the flame therein and behold the arc ascend into the center of the Divine Monad. Now take your right hand and dip it into the fires of your heart and draw the circle of our oneness around yourselves as you stand in adoration of the One. Visualize this circle, twelve feet in diameter, as a line of sacred fire. It is your ring-pass-not. Within that circle of oneness is the forcefield of Alpha and Omega; and you focus the T'ai chi, the plus and minus of cosmic energies, where you are.

Let the flow of your love be not in imitation of the idolatrous generation. Let it not be the mechanization of sex as the Luciferians have popularized their sordid and sadistic ways. The flow of the Holy Spirit twixt father and mother is for the birth of the Divine Manchild, first within each heart and then in the Bethlehem babe. Seek not the thrills of sensuality or the titillation of mind or body, but seek the bliss of mutual reunion in the Presence.

Let your love be the reenactment of the alchemical marriage. Let your love be consecrated for the soul's ultimate reunion with the I AM Presence. So is the marriage ritual intended to be the rehearsal for the great drama of your soul's assumption into the flame of love for the rolling-up of the scroll of identity into the Great Silence of your own I AM THAT I AM and for the fusion of those twin flames of the Godhead when the I AM Presence of each half of the Divine Whole merges in the hallowed circle of God.

Seek the bliss of the raising of the Mother light—of *sushumna, ida,* and *pingala*[4]—as these form the caduceus energies that reveal your real identity in Christ. Let your bliss transcend the earthly senses, and let your light flow from all of the chakras to reinforce the divine polarity of the Father-Mother God in every level of consciousness to be outpictured in the seven major chakras and the five chakras of the secret rays.

Your marriage is made in heaven and you are wed to God. Daughters of the flame: Behold, thy Maker is thine husband.[5] So be, with Mary, the handmaid of the Lord.[6] Sons of the flame: The golden band you wear is the halo of the Cosmic Virgin, the bride descending out of heaven[7] to consummate your love on earth.

As above, so below, the cosmic flow of Father-Mother God is intended to be shared in the sanctuary of the Holy Family. And it is intended to be sealed with the blessing of the true ministers of the Logos and to be guarded by purity in the holy of holies. The ark of the covenant[8] is also a matrix of the protection of twin flames joined together in holy matrimony for a life of service to God and man. And the covering cherubim[9] must be invoked daily, for they are the guardians of love in the planes of Mater.

Understand, O wise ones pursuing the law of the Logos, that if the fallen ones can destroy love, they can destroy all. For love is the foundation and the fountain of life. Love is the essence of creation. Without love, life is desolate and the skies are dreary and elemental life is despondent.

Where the love of father, mother, and child is broken, as in the totalitarian state, there is a depression that hangs over the land. And to compensate therefor, the people engage in a fierce rationalization of dialectical materialism. Without love the justifications of unreality are piled upon justification, and the impenetrable wall of self-deception that is erected, stone upon stone, of the hardness of their hearts is sealed with the mortar of their rejection of the God of love.

And so the superstate is built as the tower of Babel was built.[10] And men and women are saturated with an enormous pride in the ego and its accomplishments—

all of this to stifle the aching in the soul, the aching for the tenderness of love, the caress of father, of mother, a humble home—a hearth kindled in the fires of Father, Son, and Holy Spirit, an abode we can call our own, a creativity won by the work of our hands, the distillations of our minds, a sacred labor perfected by striving and surrender unto love.

Let them build their towers to the sky! Let them erect a monolith to the ego! Let them train their armies, forge their weapons, plan their destructions! They are on a collision course with cosmic destiny, and the end of their rationalization of unreality is self-destruction. The intensification of the fire of love will consume all of this. As surely as the rod of heaven is thrust into the ground of Terra, as surely as judgment is come, as surely as the golden vial of the wrath of mankind's misuse of love is poured out among the nations, so will come the undoing of all mankind's wrongdoing.

It was the release of the intense action of our love that confounded the language of those who sought to build a monument to mammon. And the Lord God, through the Archangel and Archeia of the Third Ray, "scattered them abroad from thence upon the face of all the earth," and they left off the building of their city and their tower. And it was called Babel, for their rationalization became as the babbling of voices who have not the understanding of the heart.

Love begins at home. Love must be enshrined in the home and at the altar of the true Church. Love must be ensouled in the nation and in the world community. For if love is not raised up by the children of the One to consume all evil on Terra, then love will descend out of heaven as the chastening fires of the Holy Ghost; and none shall escape the cataclysm that will ensue.

This is the choice which Saint Germain has set

before you. Choose love this day, and live in love and live peacefully in the land that the Lord God has given unto you. Choose love, and you will prosper and all will go well. Choose the hallowed circle of the Father-Mother God and find there succor from the crassness of the world and surcease from all struggle.

Choose love this day and live, for the fire of love descending out of the heavens will surely come to implement the judgment ere the cycles of the century have turned. And those who are in the circle of oneness will receive those fires as the gentle rain of the Spirit, but those who are outside will experience love as the fire descending as brimstone from the mountain of the Lord.

By love civilizations have risen; by love they have fallen. In love is the all-power of Brahma, Vishnu, and Shiva—the Creator, the Preserver, and the Destroyer. See, then, that you have respect for love; for love in its omnipotence is the fulfilling of the law of sacred being.

I AM

Charity

in the veil of the Cosmic Virgin

THE FOURTH VIAL

VII

THE JUDGMENT OF THE SUN

The Fourth Vial

Children of the One Who Would Enter
the Flaming Presence of the Dawn:

I come forth from the white-fire core of the Great Central Sun! I step out of the fires of the dawn, and my angels with me. We come kissed by the golden pink glow ray. The fires of love and purity, as dewdrop and crystal, flow from our garments as we traverse the morning with the angels of the dawn.

Children of the sun, I would that you would become worshipers of the dawn and of the sun. For in your meditation upon the rising orb of Helios and Vesta, you face the East and behold the rising Christ and the consciousness thereof illumining a darkened world. And you see in the fire that pierces the night with the morning light the image of your own I AM Presence. You glimpse the brilliance in physical, tangible manifestation of the I AM THAT I AM.

So dazzling is the sun of God that mortal eyes can scarcely focus upon that concentrated energy. And the rays of the sun, as they filter through the impurities of the atmosphere, can be harmful to body, soul, and mind. Yet this is but a fragment of the I AM Presence focused in time and space to awaken your soul memory of the Infinite One. Such a minute fraction of your own God-reality is this center of your solar system, can you imagine what it would be like to see the sun behind the sun, your own I AM Presence? To visualize the replica focused so lovingly and tenderly, so tangibly by Helios and Vesta is enough to increase in a moment your perception of inner spheres.

Therefore, you see, I would that you would become worshipers of the dawn, that you might carry with you throughout the day the God consciousness of your God-reality and never for a moment forget as you walk the strait and narrow path[1] to your ascension that hovering very near is the great dazzling sun of your own I AM Presence releasing limitless light and energy, the abundance of every good and perfect gift of wisdom and love and power and the many mansions of the Father's house[2] that are lowered even now into physical manifestation for the enshrining of the flame of the Mother.

Yes, I come for the judgment; but I look beyond the judgment. And I see through the crystal of the mind of God—and not in the crystal ball of the psychic moon-gazers—beyond the crucifixion, beyond the fiery cross of trial and tribulation, the hour of the resurrection of the sons and daughters of God. Yes, I see the way clearly marked. I see the way of the overcomers who walk into the light of the dawn, who are not content to bask in the light of the Presence, but who follow that light with the intensity of an absolute God-determination to return to the One.

Children of the One, we shall deliver the golden vial unto the generations of Terra—but not before we have stood in the presence of every son and daughter of God, every child of light on Terra. For I am the angel of the annunciation. Therefore I announce to you your virgin birth in the womb of the Cosmic Virgin. I announce to you that you are of the seed of Alpha, that you have been sired by Almighty God, that you have been nourished by the fires of the heart of Omega, and that you have been set for the fall and rising again of many in Israel and for a sign, which is the sign of the Logos, which shall be spoken against.[3] You have been sent into this world—although you are not of this world—as instruments of the Lord's judgment, even as you have come to balance the scales of your own uses and misuses of God's energy.

Let the violet flame go before me! Let it fall from the heavens as the lightning and the thunder of the Holy Spirit! Let it rise from the fountains of the deep[4] and from the sun of even pressure in the heart of the earth. Let the undulations of the violet flame now pave the way for the annunciation of the purity of the soul before the souls of the light-bearers are surrounded with the darkness that must surely come before the light of the dawn.

Do not question my word. For in the moment when you read this communication from on high, sent and signified by the messenger of the Lord, you will know that I am standing in your presence. And if you will close your eyes and meditate upon the sun centered within your heart, you will receive the flow of purity from my causal body and the golden pink glow ray of the angels of my band.

Take then this *Pearl of Wisdom* and read it again and again. At the hour and the moment of the dawn, face the East as the Muhammadans do. And let your prayers be unto the Christ in all mankind and unto the universal Christ; and know that in that moment of communion, the purity of your soul is reinforced for the battle in the Dark Cycle.

Know this, O chela of the law, that I can and I shall come to you in the first fiery glimmer of the dawn that is the hope of the resurrection of the son of God.

As surely as I came to Anna and Joachim to announce the birth of the child Mary,[5] as surely as I came to Elisabeth and Zacharias to proclaim the coming of John the Baptist,[6] as surely as I went before the virgin to announce the birth of the Saviour,[7] so I shall stand before you—not only to speak the word of the birth of your soul in the flaming spirit of the resurrection, but also to transfer from my flaming aura to your own the energies of the Great Central Sun in the white-fire core of life.

Let my presence pierce the veil of skepticism and cynicism and the endless human questioning—questioning even the very existence of the archangels and the angelic host. What blasphemy against the Lord God himself to deny the existence of the angels who personify the great feelings of the Almighty for the creation biding in the planes of Mater!

I am Gabriel; and I come with Hope, my own divine complement, in the flame of our joint mission. Our hope for the restoration of the souls of the fallen ones is never for a moment set aside. As long as there is life and even the flickering of the flame of life upon the altar of the heart, we breathe the breath of the Holy Spirit upon that life, upon that flame, fanning the flame with renewal, directing the consciousness to new horizons.

Each day is a day of hope—hope for resurrection, hope for the setting of the records straight, for the clearing of the fire body (repository of the blueprint of the divine plan), the clearing of the etheric envelope of all of the sordid or supercilious aspects of human life. I should say human existence; for those who inhabit the veils of mortality, gray and shadowed, that keep the consciousness in a perpetual state of mourning, of complaining, of a sense of loss and of the sense that life is not meting out the just portion, those who dwell in the semi-state of awareness of the True Self—these truly have not yet begun to live. They have only a quasi-existence that remains to be quickened by the fires of the Holy Spirit.

Let the trumpets of the archangels sound and let the dead be raised incorruptible! For the human consciousness shall be changed. And this that is corruptible man must put on the incorruption of the Divine Man. Therefore, in this hour of the judgment, let this mortal put on immortality.[8] This is my annunciation and this is the electrode of my life which I transfer to you—you who would be light-bearers to the age.

Now when you practice the ritual of the opening of the door of the heart which was told to you by the Archeia Christine and you receive the Mother and the initiations of Maitreya through the Mother and you receive me, Gabriel, an archangel, in the name of the Lord, you will begin the transformation through the stations of the cross and the initiations of the transfiguration, the crucifixion, the resurrection, and the ascension. And you will proclaim with the endless voices of the heavenly hosts who come in celebration of your victory:

"So when this corruptible shall have put on incorruption and this mortal shall have put on immortality, then shall be brought to pass the saying that is written, Death is swallowed up in victory. O death, where is thy sting? O grave, where is thy victory? The sting of death is sin; and the strength of sin is the law. But thanks be to God, which giveth us the victory through our Lord Jesus Christ."[9]

Now the moment is come, and the fourth angel descending from the Temple of the Tabernacle of the Testimony doth pour out his vial upon the sun [upon the etheric plane, the plane of the fire element], and power is given unto him to scorch men with fire. And this is the sacred fire by which mankind are scorched with a great heat, so much so that they blaspheme the name of God, the Almighty One, the only one who hath power over these plagues. And therefore, as it is written, they repented not to give him glory.[10]

Stand fast, then, to behold the salvation of our God![11] And behold the death of the wicked[12] and of the generations of the wicked. For the fallen ones and their carnal creation are brought to naught on that notable day of the Lord—the day of the release of the sacred fire.

I am the archangel of ascension's fires. I stand in the brilliance of the noonday to counteract the midnight hour. I stand before the throne of God to intercede before the Lord God Almighty on behalf of those who blaspheme his name. I shield his throne from the echoings of mankind's infamy. And the thundering and the lightning that descend from Horeb[13] are a warning unto mankind to walk away from evil, to leave it in the way, to depart from the evildoers, to separate themselves bodily from those who have made themselves the instruments of unrighteousness and channels for the pollutions of the psychic realm.

What fellowship hath righteousness with unrighteousness? And what communion hath light with darkness?[14] Do not allow the sympathy of the Luciferians to prey upon the very light of your soul! Do not allow your consciousness to be entertained by the so-called sorrows of Satan! Do not feel sorry for those who do evil; for they, too, have the option of walking away from their evil ways.

But go rather to the lost sheep of the house of Israel[15] to proclaim the name of God—the power by which all souls yet tarrying in time and space can be saved. Proclaim the coming of the Christed ones and rebuke the devils who usurp the pure energies of the Mother and of the Holy Spirit. See how your love, replacing all sympathy, will go forth as the compassion of the law to compel the children of God who tarry in their childish ways to rise to the standard of the Christ.

I am an archangel—and I survey the consciousness of the light-bearers. And I am choosing the most stalwart and the most self-disciplined ones for the front lines of the battle of Armageddon. Let us see who will be the forerunners in the race for the light of the dawn.

I am Gabriel. My shield is Hope, my sword is Faith, and my thrust is Charity. I am the Word of God in manifestation throughout cosmos.

I leave you with the words of the great preacher "Therefore, my beloved brethren, be ye stedfast, unmoveable, always abounding in the work of the Lord, forasmuch as ye know that your labour is not in vain in the Lord."[16]

"Behold, I come quickly," saith the Lord.[17]

Gabriel

of the Sun

VIII

DELIVERANCE FROM THE HARSHNESS OF THE JUDGMENT

The Raising of the Right Hand of the Mother

Children of the One Standing in the Light of Hope:

Indeed may you be grateful that God has sent forth a ray of hope unto the evolutions of this world. And I am grateful to ensoul that ray that you might pursue it to the fiery core of your own blueprint. Standing in the presence of your own I AM THAT I AM, you may renew the ancient covenant of your soul with your Maker to be the fullness of the law of disciplined love, to be the conscious outpouring of the flow of Mother, to be the two-edged sword of Alpha keeping the way of the Tree of Life,[1] setting the example of purity to an age.

I am the angel immaculate. From the snowy peaks of Shasta, from the Himalayas and the Rockies, I send forth the piercing light of purity which unfortunately reveals the aberrations of the divine plan as well as the soul's immaculate conception in the heart of God. Purity reveals all. Hope, too, is a two-edged sword releasing the intensity of God-reality that brings forth the anguish of the soul as it beholds line upon line its departure from divinity.

I come with the warning of the archangels; and I say to all: Repent in the name of the Lord! There is no turning back on the path of salvation, for there is no turning back of the cycles of karma once they are released. Therefore Jesus admonished, "No man, having put his hand to the plough, and looking back, is fit for the kingdom of God."[2] Those who begin the ascent, the arduous climb to the highest summit, must not turn back when initiation confronts them in the way; for the alternative to passing every test and submitting to every initiation is to be subject unto the concentrated release of one's own karma.

More greatly to be feared than the tests and the trials of the Path is the outer darkness that comes when the soul deserts the flame, deserts the battlefield of the Lord for that most questionable of all human commodities—human comfort. In outer darkness all is chaos, disorder, and disintegration. There the meting-out of karma measure by measure that comes from the Lords of Karma through the hand of the master and the Christ Self into the crucible of the chela is no longer a grace that can be counted on.

When you turn your back on the flame, you can count on nothing. The dispensations of mercy and opportunity dispensed at the hand of the Lords of Karma are not the option of the fallen ones or of the children of God who have fallen from grace. Who will intercede for them when they say to the mountains and rocks, "Fall on us, and hide us from the face of him that sitteth on the throne and from the wrath of the Lamb: for the great day of his wrath is come; and who shall be able to stand?"[3] To turn one's back on the flame is to forfeit the intercession of the great Mediator of life.

Take heed, then, all who would run and not be weary, all who have set their mark on "the prize of the high calling of God in Christ Jesus."[4] The race is to those who will run to the finish; and those who are not prepared to go all the way had better not start, for the price for desertion is far too great. The covenants of God and the blessings of the ascended masters and their messengers are not to be trifled with.

Let us see, then, how the Lords of Karma compassionately allow the soul to balance the mastery of personal karma with the carrying of a portion of the weight of planetary karma. Those who are diligent in the application of the law and in their daily invocations to the flames of the sacred fire have nothing to fear; for they are moving in and through the returning cycles of personal and planetary karma as they stand, face, and conquer every erg of energy that diverges from the center of life.

Stand holding the two-edged sword with both hands. Clasp it directly in front of you and let the blade cut the oncoming tide of darkness in defense of the light of the heart. Let it part the wave of the Dark Cycle and let it redirect those energies into the sacred fires burning on the altar of the Mother. Her flame is the flame of purity. It is the all-consuming fire of the Holy Spirit; for the Mother is the Bride of the Holy Spirit, and unto her is given the allness of the sacred fire necessary for the consuming of the karma of the seven last plagues.

What must mankind do to merit the intercession of the Mother? For she is the instrument of the Lord; she is the receptacle into which the power of his name "I AM THAT I AM" does flow. And therefore on earth the Mother is the instrument of the judgment that proceeds from the Father in heaven. Pay homage to her Son, the Christ of all, and acknowledge the source—the Woman clothed with the Sun and the womb of the Cosmic Virgin out of which issues the flaming Sun Presence of all.

When mankind shall receive the Mother in the name of the Father, in the name of the Son, and in the name of the Holy Spirit, then they will have unlimited access to the flowing fountain of her purity, her all-consuming love. And then the woes that are presently coming upon mankind shall be stopped by the raising of the right hand of the Mother, by the power of the spoken Word, by the wisdom of the scepter of her authority, by the love of the crown of her overcoming.

Therefore, let the children of God repent this day in the name of the Lord! Let them find refuge in the Mother and in the Mother flame. Let them give the recitation of the Hail Mary[5] as a means of their atonement for the sins of mankind, and let their meditation on the Mother ray be for the raising of the light of the white-fire core for the detoxification of bodies and souls and minds of the wraths of the seven last plagues.

Now hear the word of the preacher: "To every thing there is a season, and a time to every purpose under the heaven. A time to be born and a time to die; a time to plant and a time to pluck up that which is planted; a time to kill and a time to heal; a time to break down and a time to build up; a time to weep and a time to laugh; a time to mourn and a time to dance."[6]

This is the time to be serious, to take to heart the principles and the precepts of the law and the training you have received from the ascended masters and their messengers. This is the time to invoke the flame of Sirius, the God Star, to invoke the counsel of the Four and Twenty Elders and the intercession of Surya and the angels of Sirius, who descend in answer to your call in the formation of a great blue eagle.

Take then the call to Surya[7] which I have directed should be included with this *Pearl of Wisdom,* and let it be shouted from the housetops! Let it be sent forth from all of your chakras with the utmost adoration to God, with the utmost humility and the utmost concentration of the sacred fire within your chakras. Let nothing take from you your commitment to this call, for it will deliver you from the toils of the toiler and from the harshness of the judgment. And it will deliver the wicked into the hands of the legions from Sirius.

Let the fallen ones with their satanic rites tremble! Let those who have mutilated the cattle on the plains of America know that the judgment is nigh! They are broken this day by the rod of Almighty God! Let those who defend their rites of black magic and witchcraft also know that judgment is nigh, for you cannot take the purity of the Divine Mother and use it for selfish motive.

Each interference with the free will of God and man exacts the penalty of the law and of the Lawgiver. There are those who say in their hearts: "Let us do evil that good may come.[8] Let us compromise the teaching of the ascended masters. Let us go around the Christ and enter the Lord's house at the side door. Let us convince mankind that we are practicing the divine art. Let us prove by distortion of the Mother flame that our way is the acceptable way." These gather in their covens and in their dens of iniquity professing to serve the light. I say, they have usurped the light and they shall pay the price. "There shall be weeping and gnashing of teeth."

And these wizards
That have come out of the astral night
Convince their followers,
By the appearance of right,
That their way is of the light.
Beware appearances!
Beware the "way that seemeth right."[9]
Relative good and evil afford no proof
Of Absolute Truth.
Only the law of just cause
Can produce the certain effect
Of the Holy Spirit
Who comes with healing in his wings.[10]
Put aside these other things,

These incantations that reek
With the stench of perversion
And the decaying bodies of children
And animals they have slain.
Beware of all that is vain
And the vanity of the ego.
More deadly than the Fallen One himself
Is the rot of the ego
That is transplanted from body to body,
From mind to mind,
As a cancer that eats away
To the very soul of a planet and a people.

Let us be the instruments of righteous judgment! Let us tether the souls of mankind to the holy of holies! Let us weave the garment of the Lord that the children of Israel may pass over the Red Sea stained by the blood of the holy innocents.[11] Yes, let them pass over from the planes of Mater to the planes of Spirit, from the corruptible to the Incorruptible One; and let those who have the intent to murder the Divine Mother be judged by their motive this day. Let their hatred of the flame of Aquarius be turned upon them by the raising of the hand of the Mother and of the scepter of her authority!

For the Lord is come down to judge the earth this day, he who "doeth great things past finding out; yea, and wonders without number. Lo, he goeth by me, and I see him not: he passeth on also, but I perceive him not. Behold, he taketh away, who can hinder him? who will say unto him, What doest thou?"[12]

I AM

Hope

Archeia of the Fourth Ray of Purity

I command purity
and I am purity's judgment in this cycle.

THE FIFTH VIAL

IX

THE JUDGMENT OF THE CARNAL MIND AS THE SEAT OF AUTHORITY IN MATER

The Fifth Vial

Children of the One Who Would Light a Candle
in the Night, Hail!

Hail to the flaming ones who fear not to stand in the presence of truth! I am the Archangel of the Fifth Ray, and my coming marks the intensification of judgment in Mater; for the fifth ray is the ray of precipitation. And when the chemist in his laboratory combines sodium and chlorine, invariably there is a chemical reaction and the precipitation of salt.

And so it is with the flame of truth. It brings all things to the fore of consciousness—the elements of the mind and of the emotions, the substance of the subconscious as well as physical densities. When the ray of truth is used as the catalyst, that which is unseen becomes the seen. And the disobedience of Lot's wife precipitates the pillar of salt,[1] that all who seek to raise up the feminine ray might know that obedience is the key to godly alchemy.

The approbation of the heavenly will
The law of righteousness does instill
In all who would now prove the truth.

Stand forth, the soul, as living proof!
Come out from among them
And be a separate people![2]

Let the light-bearers themselves
Be the precipitation of the Christ!
Let them, by the catalyst of the inner flame,
Send forth the call of the I AM name.
Let them precede the day of judgment
To apply the law of self-perfectionment.
Let them precipitate the good and the noble
Ere sacred fire reveal the evil and ignoble.
Let all choose and choose well
Ere choice is no longer in the hand of man,
But in the hand of God.
Choose to be and you will see
The angel with the flaming sword.
In the right hand is life;
In the left is death.
Choose you this day whom ye will serve;[3]
Your lot shall be as you deserve.

I come forth from the Temple of the Tabernacle of the Testimony. And the heavens are opened this day as I pour out from the golden vial the wrath of God upon the seat of the beast; and his kingdom is full of darkness this day; and those that worship the beast shall gnaw their tongues for pain and blaspheme the God of heaven because of their pains and their sores; yet they repent not of their deeds.[4]

This vial contains mankind's wrathful misuses of the fifth ray of life and the science of life, of healing and healing truth, and of the abundance of the immaculate consciousness of the Cosmic Virgin. All of this the fallen ones have taken to create the beast of the carnal mind sitting in the seat of the soul. Now we unseat the carnal mind! We dislodge it from its moorings! We cut it off from the light of the soul! No longer shall it vampirize the solar energies of the sons and daughters of God. It has laid claim to earthly existence. Let it stand this day before the Court of the Sacred Fire and present proof of its origin, its lineage, its heritage.

Let those who rely on the carnal mind as the seat of a human authority and a human personality prepare themselves to give testimony before the Four and Twenty Elders. Let them receive our warning that all that proceeds out of the light of the Logos and all that is of God, showing forth allegiance to Alpha and Omega, will live in the eternal kingdom. And all that is of the world must receive the judgment of this world.

I place the light of living truth as a sphere of the immaculate conception around the souls of the children of God who are loyal to their Creator in the last days. Let their souls and the dwelling place of their souls in the chakra of freedom be sealed in the light of the Mother ray and of the archeia of the new day. For the souls of mankind have been literally squashed by the beast who is bound this day by the seven archangels. And we hold back the beast to make way for the coming into prominence of the souls of mankind, that they might have the freedom in the flame of Saint Germain, hierarch of the Aquarian age, to choose the light, to choose the right, and to be centered in the God flame.

And therefore while Satan is bound for a thousand years at the Court of the Sacred Fire, so the counterpart of Satan, which is the carnal mind of each one and the very presence of antichrist that challenges the soul day and night, is also bound, that mankind might exercise free will in the flame of freedom without interference from the darkened self, the shadowed self, the not-self. Therefore this day is the influence of the carnal mind stayed on Terra in the consciousness of the children of God!

Given the freedom to choose, they may still choose the ego and the self-centered existence. So be it. We will not interfere with free will. We come as intercessors of the law responding to the calls of the Faithful and True. For the Lord Christ himself, as the Good Shepherd of the sheep,[5] has knelt before the altar of the Most High God, praying fervently as he did through the long night in Gethsemane for the Lord's intercession on behalf of the sheep.[6]

Therefore we come fulfilling the dispensations of the Almighty granted unto the beloved Son. We come to intensify the all-seeing eye, to give mankind the vision of the choice, to lock the souls in the flame of truth that can make them free[7] if they will to be free. But the fallen ones with their robot creation have not the dispensation of the children of God, for they are the seed of the Evil One. And for some the end is not yet come,[8] and for some the day of reckoning is at hand.

And they stagger and they stalk the earth, and they glower as they hover in their spacecraft. And not all are of this planetary home. And some are a physical evolution and others inhabit the astral plane. And some have not been allowed to incarnate in tens of thousands of years; for by the intercession of the Lord Christ, they have been confined to the dungeons of the astral, bound in chains—yes, bound hand and foot. But the abomination of their carnality is the contamination of Mater. Thus far and no farther! The day of judgment comes in the year of the Holy Spirit, nineteen hundred and seventy-five; and the day of judgment continues to the year two thousand and one.

And there is yet time and space for every man and woman and child upon Terra to partake of the Eucharist, to assimilate the body and the blood, the Omega and the Alpha spirals of the Christ consciousness. And there is yet time and space for the message of the two witnesses to cover the earth if the lightbearers will be diligent as runners of the gods carrying the message from house to house, from nation to nation, stopping only for sustenance and brief periods of rest under the wings of the Holy Spirit.

Children of the One, remember the darkness of the city of Jerusalem. Remember that it was so intense that the Lord Christ would not lay his body to rest in that city. And did he not exclaim, "The foxes have holes and the birds of the air have nests; but the Son of man hath not where to lay his head"?[9] Where can the sons and daughters of God go to find respite from the machinations of the dark ones? They inhabit every plane of Mater, and the thick smoke of their burnt offerings is obnoxious to the children of the One.

As the Lord Christ took refuge in the ship on the Sea of Galilee, or in the mountains, or in the home of Mary and Martha at Bethany, so you, too, can take refuge even in the planes of Mater, securing your soul in the secret place of the Most High. And remember, when judgment draweth nigh, the words of the Psalmist "Whither shall I go from thy Spirit? or whither shall I flee from thy presence? If I ascend up into heaven, thou art there: if I make my bed in hell, behold, thou art there. If I take the wings of the morning and dwell in the uttermost parts of the sea, even there shall thy hand lead me and thy right hand shall hold me."[10]

While the souls of mankind prepare to make right choices, the structures and the superstructures of the fallen ones come tumbling down; for their foundation was in the seat of the beast, whose kingdom is filled with darkness. Let the false practitioners of the healing arts be exposed! And let them repent of their deeds. Let the moneychangers in the banking houses of the world be exposed! And let them repent of their deeds. Let the ray of action penetrate the misuses of the science of precipitation! And let all that has been precipitated out of the astral plane, out of the collective subconscious, out of the seat of the beast, be challenged by the sword of truth! And the Great Divine Director comes forth to arrest the spirals of the misuses of the Christ light in the seven rays of God.[11]

Behold, mankind, now is the accepted time! Now is the day of salvation! Now let those who are contributing to the pollution of the body of the Mother through the manufacture and sale of alcohol, cigarettes, marijuana, and every harmful drug be exposed! And let them repent of their deeds. Let the selling of sex and the promotion of products accompanied by subliminal sex symbols be exposed! And let those with bloodstained hands repent of their deeds.

I reinforce the judgment of abortion and the abortionist delivered by Almighty God through the pronouncement of the Archangel Uriel.[12] And I send forth my ray into the houses of whoredom where the flame of the Mother is being desecrated and the Eves of this world are daily tempting Adam-man to partake of the forbidden fruit of the tree of the knowledge of good and evil. Let them be exposed! And let them repent of their deeds.

In the name of the I AM THAT I AM, I send forth the fires of the crystal ray! And there shall come upon mankind suddenly, without warning, a freezing of their actions and their consciousness as on the day that the sun and the moon stood still[13] and the stars themselves were fixed in their courses. So for a moment of eternity slipped into time and space, there shall be a silence and all action shall be brought to a halt; and the angels of the Lord shall take note of the deeds of mankind and of the fallen ones.

And there will not be time for the people to put on their Sunday best and to primp and to preen before the mirrors of their vanity. This is the Lord's "candid camera." And the shutter of the all-seeing eye of God will click, and the soul will hear the click, and the fallen ones will hear the click, and they will know that the evidence has been taken for the execution of the judgment this day.

Be diligent, O my children—children of the One! Work the works of righteousness, fulfill the law of life taught by the Christed ones, and fear not. For those who fulfill their sacred vows have nothing to fear, but only the anticipation of joy, liberation, light, and discovery that comes on the wings of judgment—the judgment that shall surely be known as the greatest manifestation of love that the world has ever known.

I AM

Raphael

Defender of the Virgin Mother
and of the Ma-ray within you

I stand on the east side of the City Foursquare.

YOUR DIVINE SELF

Chart of Your Divine Self

There are three figures represented in the chart, which we will refer to as the upper figure, the middle figure, and the lower figure. The upper figure is the I AM Presence, the I AM THAT I AM, God individualized for every son and daughter of God. The Divine Monad consists of the I AM Presence surrounded by the spheres (rings of color, of light) which comprise the causal body. This is the body of First Cause that contains within it man's "treasure laid up in heaven"—perfect works, perfect thoughts and feelings, perfect words—energies that have ascended from the plane of action in time and space as the result of man's correct exercise of free will and his correct qualification of the stream of life that issues forth from the heart of the Presence and descends to the level of the Christ Self.

The middle figure in the chart is the mediator between God and man, called the Christ Self, the Real Self, or the Christ consciousness. It has also been referred to as the Higher Mental Body or Higher Consciousness. The Christ Self overshadows the lower self, which consists of the soul evolving through the four planes of Matter in the four lower bodies corresponding to the planes of earth, air, fire, and water; that is, the etheric body, the mental body, the emotional body, the physical body.

The three figures of the chart correspond to the Trinity of Father (the upper figure), Son (the middle figure), and Holy Spirit. The lower figure is intended to become the temple for the Holy Spirit which is indicated in the enfolding violet-flame action of the sacred fire. The lower figure corresponds to you as a disciple on the Path. Your soul is the nonpermanent aspect of being which is made permanent through the ritual of the ascension. The ascension is the process whereby the soul, having balanced his karma and fulfilled his divine plan, merges first with the Christ consciousness and then with the living Presence of the I AM THAT I AM. Once the ascension has taken place, the soul, the corruptible aspect of being, becomes the incorruptible one, a permanent atom in the body of God. The Chart of Your Divine Self is therefore a diagram of yourself—past, present, and future.

The lower figure represents mankind evolving in the planes of Matter. This is how you should visualize yourself standing in the violet flame, which you invoke in the name of the I AM Presence and in the name of your Christ Self in order to purify your four lower bodies in preparation for the ritual of the alchemical marriage—your soul's union with the Lamb as the bride of Christ. The lower figure is surrounded by a tube of light, which is projected from the heart of the I AM Presence in answer to your call. It is a field of fiery protection sustained in Spirit and in Matter for the sealing of the individuality of the disciple. The threefold flame within the heart is the spark of life projected from the I AM Presence through the Christ Self and anchored in the etheric planes in the heart chakra for the purpose of the soul's evolution in Matter. Also called the Christ flame, the threefold flame is the spark of man's divinity, his potential for Godhood.

The crystal cord is the stream of light that descends from the heart of the I AM Presence through the Christ Self, thence to the four lower bodies to sustain the soul's vehicles of expression in time and space. It is over this cord that the energy of the Presence flows, entering the being of man at the top of the head and providing the energy for the pulsation of the threefold flame and the physical heartbeat. When a round of the soul's incarnation in Matter-form is complete, the I AM Presence withdraws the crystal cord, the threefold flame returns to the level of the Christ, and the energies of the four lower bodies return to their respective planes.

The dove of the Holy Spirit descending from the heart of the Father is shown just above the head of the Christ. When the individual man, as the lower figure, puts on and becomes the Christ consciousness as Jesus did, the descent of the Holy Spirit takes place and the words of the Father, the I AM Presence, are spoken, "This is my beloved Son in whom I AM well pleased" (Matt. 3:17).

A more detailed explanation of the Chart of Your Divine Self is given in the Keepers of the Flame Lessons and in *Climb the Highest Mountain* by Mark L. Prophet and Elizabeth Clare Prophet, published by Summit University Press.

Our son, Micah, Angel of Unity, encircles the earth, traversing the lines of longitude. He with his angels of unity carry the flaming sword to slay the dragons roaming the continents of the mind to divide and conquer the body of God upon earth.

—Archeia Faith

My sword is thrust into the ground, and it transmits the rod of fire from the altar of the Most High God! And the atoms of the earth do quiver and tremble as the electrode of Almighty God brings into alignment light with light, darkness with darkness, that it might be no more, that death might be swallowed up in victory.

—Archangel Uriel

You call me the Queen of Angels, and I have so been made by God because I have descended for a little time lower than the archeiai into the planes of mater-realization; and thereby by the overcoming of the Holy Spirit, I have been crowned with more glory and honor.

—Archeia Mary

And I read the proclamation that comes from the hand of Alpha and Omega this day. It is a proclamation of opportunity in grace for your soul to return to paradise lost, to the garden of the causal body, to the place where the consciousness of the Christ implants the knowledge of the tree of the knowledge of good and evil. . . .

I am the flaming presence of the Christed one! I stand before you, yet I am in the center of the sun! I am the living presence of the flame—mine to have and yours to claim.

—Archangel Uriel

The approbation of the heavenly will
The law of righteousness does instill
In all who would now prove the truth.
Stand forth, the soul, as living proof!
Come out from among them
And be a separate people!

Let the light-bearers themselves
Be the precipitation of the Christ!
Let them, by the catalyst of the inner flame,
Send forth the call of the I AM name.
Let them precede the day of judgment
To apply the law of self-perfectionment.
Let them precipitate the good and the noble
Ere sacred fire reveal the evil and ignoble.
Let all choose and choose well
Ere choice is no longer in the hand of man,
But in the hand of God.
Choose to be and you will see
The angel with the flaming sword.

—*Archangel Raphael*

Auriel Bessemer

It is time to light the torch of the age of freedom. . . .

I set my seal upon the fire and upon the air, upon the waters and upon the earth.

—*Archeia Amethyst*

Auriel Bessemer

I am the angel who talked with John. And I showed him that woman sitting "upon the scarlet-colored beast, full of names of blasphemy, having seven heads and ten horns," that woman "arrayed in purple and scarlet color and decked with gold and precious stones and pearls, having a golden cup in her hand full of abominations and filthiness of her fornication." And John saw the name written upon her forehead: "MYSTERY, BABYLON THE GREAT, THE MOTHER OF HARLOTS AND ABOMINATIONS OF THE EARTH." And he saw "the woman drunken with the blood of the saints and with the blood of the martyrs of Jesus." And I told him that the waters which he saw where the whore sitteth, even the waters of the great river, are the peoples and multitudes and nations and tongues who gave their energies to Babylon the great.

—Archangel Uriel

Harriet Bessemer

Let those who march with the Divine Mother carrying the banner of Maitreya, the Cosmic Christ, call forth the sacred fire from their own causal bodies of light, from the I AM THAT I AM, to consume the cause and core of the disintegration and the death that is the record of the murder of the Divine Mother and the slaughter of the holy innocents that has been enacted again and again on Lemuria, on Atlantis, and in every civilization ancient and modern where the fallen ones have moved in with their darkness and their deviltry, their degradation of the image of the Woman and their degeneration of the energies of the children of the light.

Now comes the judgment of the fallen ones! And with the descent of the fires of judgment none are spared. . . .

I am Michael, Prince of the Archangels. I stand on the side of the north of the City Foursquare, and my right hand is raised to release the light of the Presence. In the words of Alpha I say, "Children of the One: Forge your God-identity!"

—Archangel Michael

I stand on the side of the west of the City Foursquare. I stand on the West Coast of the United States of America. And I face the East and the kings and queens of the East to gather them to the battle of that great day of God Almighty. I raise my hands for the release of the momentum of the violet flame that shall reverse the tide of darkness and roll it back from the West unto the East. And it shall be as the rolling-up of a mighty scroll, and it shall be the rolling-up of that darkness which has covered the land. And it shall be the rolling-up of the unclean spirits that, like frogs, have been sent forth out of the mouth of the dragon and out of the mouth of the beast and out of the mouth of the false prophet.

—Archangel Zadkiel

I am the angel immaculate. From the snowy peaks of Shasta, from the Himalayas and the Rockies, I send forth the piercing light of purity. . . . Purity reveals all. Hope, too, is a two-edged sword that brings forth the anguish of the soul as it beholds line upon line its departure from divinity.

I come with the warning of the archangels; and I say to all: Repent in the name of the Lord!

—*Archeia Hope*

Let all the world know that the Lord God omnipotent reigneth! Let the angel choirs sing the alleluia! Let the worlds rejoice! Let the stars in the heavens rejoice! Let the sons and daughters of God rejoice, for the Lord God omnipotent reigneth!

—Archeia Amethyst

As you read our admonishments set forth in these fourteen Pearls of Wisdom, let them be for your strengthening as you face the Lord Christ and his Mother and her flame and the Word incarnate. And as you prepare to receive from the Holy Spirit those sacred fires that are for the consuming of all resistance of the carnal mind to the quickening of the soul through the adversity of the cross,

Stand, face, and conquer with sword in hand
and the fire of love burning in your heart!
Stand, face, and conquer the dividing of the
waters and the vials we impart!
Stand, face, and conquer! Plunge the sword
of truth into the cause and core of the
lie.
Stand, face, and conquer! For the army of
the Lord draweth nigh.

—Archeia Aurora

X

THE CHEMICALIZATION OF TRUTH WHICH THE JUDGMENT BRINGS

Bearing the Divine Manchild

Children of the One, Come into the Sacred Heart
of the Cosmic Virgin:

In this hour of the Lord's judgment, there come to mind the words of blessed Paul "For we know that the whole creation groaneth and travaileth in pain together until now. And not only they, but ourselves also, which have the firstfruits of the Spirit, even we ourselves groan within ourselves, waiting for the adoption, to wit, the redemption of our body."[1]

Truth is the transforming power that transforms a universe. During the period of the chemicalization of truth which the judgment brings, there is the groaning and the travail like unto a mother giving birth to her firstborn son. The Christ Child is aborning within you. The judgment is the hand of God making way for the birth of the Manchild; for the forces of Herod are abroad in the land this day to prevent the birth and the maturation of the Christ flame in the hearts of humanity. Herod's men[2] come with their swords, their scalpels and their surgical instruments. They come to do the work of the dragon to devour the child as soon as it is born.

But fear not! For the warning of the angel of the Lord who appeared unto Joseph, saying, "Take the young child and his mother and flee into Egypt, and be thou there until I bring thee word; for Herod will seek the young child to destroy him"[3] comes to every son and daughter of God who has assumed the responsibility of bearing the Divine Manchild. And the angels of the Lord do intercede in this hour for the preservation of life and truth and love as the threefold flame upon the altar of the heart.

Wait and listen. Listen well to the words of the archangels and the archeiai. And read between the lines of these *Pearls of Wisdom;* for there are messages for each and every soul and there are applications for each and every circumstance contrived by the fallen ones to trap the holy innocents as they make their way over the little-traveled roads that lead to the place of safety.

I am Mary. I have chosen to ensoul the Mother ray for a cosmos. I am the handmaid of the Lord Alpha and the instrument of Omega. I am the awareness of the Father-Mother God extending even unto the planes of Mater, that the children of the One might know the sanctity of communion—of the marriage of the daughters to the Holy Spirit, of the vows of the sons unto the Cosmic Virgin.

Because the flame of the fifth ray relates to precipitation in Mater and because the feminine aspect of the flame is directly involved in the spirals of God-realization descending from the formless into form, I was chosen by Alpha and Omega to incarnate in this system of worlds, to set forth in time and space the example of the Divine Woman reaching full self-realization in and as the Divine Mother. How well I remember that moment when I was bidden by heralds of the king and queen, our own beloved Alpha and Omega, and I came escorted by the beloved Raphael to stand before the throne of the twin flames of a cosmos!

"You called, my father and my mother, and I have come."

"Yes, our beloved, we have called. Unto you and to Raphael is given the opportunity from the heart of the Solar Logoi to manifest the balance of the flow of truth 'as above, so below' over the spirals of the figure eight of our cosmos—opportunity to be on earth as in heaven the ensoulment of the Mother ray."

"What does this mean, my father and my mother?"

"It means that you have been chosen, Mary, to incarnate in the planes of Mater, to take on the feminine form which the errant souls of the children of God now wear, to live and serve among them, to adore the Christ flame within their hearts—as Sanat Kumara and Gautama have done and as the Christed ones, the avatars and Buddhas who have gone before, and the many angels who have volunteered to work through forms of flesh and blood to save the lost sheep of the house of Israel who have taken on the ways of the idolatrous generation."

I heard the words of our dearest Father-Mother and I looked into the eyes of Raphael, my beloved. And for a moment—only a moment—the pain of the anticipated separation was too much to bear. Instantly I was strengthened by the beauty and nobility of his countenance and the sternness of his eye disciplined in the law. He had, as it were, almost greater courage than I to descend into the planes of Mater.

But when I felt his hand press my own and the charge of the will of God and our dedication to eternal truth flowed into my being and soul, I faced the beloved Presence of God now pulsating in utter formlessness as cloven tongues of fire where a moment before the personages of the Divine Polarity had stood.

I knelt in utter surrender to the call of hierarchy and in silence before the Holy of Holies gave my life that the Word might become flesh and dwell among the inhabitants of Terra,[4] that the Christ, the eternal Logos, might incarnate, the Incorruptible One.[5]

Precious ones, did you know that for the souls and the angels who volunteer to incarnate in those several systems of worlds where the consciousness of the Fall, of fallen man and fallen woman, has taken over the race, there is no guarantee that the lifestream will emerge from that darkness unscathed, free to soar once more unto the arms of Everlasting Love? Those who come from heavenly octaves in defense of truth, in defense of the life of souls who have strayed from the center of being, have only their commitment to the flame to rely on—only determination and will and love. For even the memory of those other spheres must be foresworn upon entering the birth canal and assuming the body temple that has been prepared—sometimes lovingly and sometimes not so lovingly—by earthly parents.

Oh yes, God's grace is always there.
His Presence can be known.
God's love is everywhere—
Even in the wings of the morning
Where I have flown.
But, you see, it all depends upon the call
And the making of the call.
For all of the potential of God and man
Can come to naught
When souls and angels forsake the truth God brought.
The prayer, therefore, of every descending avatar
Is for the memory of the Bethlehem star,
That it might contact the teacher
And the teaching of the I AM Presence
And the Christ Self of each one

For the journey through the valleys of the earth
And then the soaring to the center of the sun.

And so I descended by God's grace;
And by his grace, and that alone,
I ascended to the heavenly throne.
Therefore I am one among the archeiai
Who have experienced directly
The veil of human tears
And the passing of the years
From darkness unto darkness
As mankind's consciousness flows
Until, quickened by some inner light,
They find the road from glory unto glory.

Take comfort, O my children!
There is not a place on earth where you can be
That I also have not been.
I have seen the tempter and the temptations of sin.
I have seen the Christ upon the cross
And held him in my arms
As infant child and by the tomb,
The moment of the consecration to the cosmic womb.
I have parted from my son along the sorrowful way
And I have seen him nailed to the cross
On a very dark day.
My soul was also pierced as yours shall be.[6]
But fear not: I am thy Mother, I AM with thee.

Because I have gone before you
In the footsteps on the Path,
Because the blessed Son
Has also descended and ascended
Throughout a cosmos vast,
You can follow in each painful, blissful footstep—
Surefooted as the mountain goat,
Leaping to your cosmic destiny
And your place upon that cross,

Hastening to greet the sword
That must pierce the soul
That you might have the compassion
To make all mankind whole.
Because the way is known,
Because we have pursued and overcome,
You who have descended in answer to the call
Of Alpha and Omega
Can be certain of ascending
If you will make your calling and election sure[7]
By the call, by the initiations,
By the testing, testing, testing.

We extend a helping hand.
Clasp it if you will!
Feel the strength of Raphael
And the sternness of his love.
Feel the assurance of the beloved
Assuring you of your attainment
According to the motto
Of those who come to do His will:[8]
You can make it if you try!
You can make it if you try!

Midst all the darkness,
The density, and the dangers
Inherent in a world scheme
Where judgment is nigh,
The archangels stand forth.
Hear their cry!
They come to intercede.
Won't you give them heed?
Their word is law
Direct from the speech of the Logos.
Their word is power manifesting the work
Of the Creator, the Preserver, the Destroyer.
In this cycle of the Holy Spirit
You can expect to hear it,

To hear the wisdom
That causes the demons to tremble[9]
And the love that is a chastening
To them who fear it.

Without the fear of the Lord
There is no repentance,
And without repentance
There can be no forgiveness.
Forgiveness flows;
But it must be invoked
By the humble of heart,
By the sincere who ask the Lord's pardon
That they might undo their wrong
And redo their right.
When the apology becomes a ritual—
Dead and without works—
Then it is better to be silent
And to engage in living sacrifice
As service to the law,
As testimony and as proof
That forgiveness is the justice
Of the mercy of the law.

When the Lord Christ, Jesus my son, prays fervently before the altar of the Most High God for the children of the One, so when I see him descending from the mountain of the Lord, "his face shining as the sun, his raiment white as the light,"[10] I run to greet him in the way and he does embrace me in the Mother ray. And then I ask him for those dispensations for the chosen ones that are his to give and mine to impart as the Matriarch of the Law.

You call me the Queen of Angels, and I have so been made by God because I have descended for a little time lower than the archeiai into the planes of Mater-realization; and thereby by the overcoming of the Holy Spirit, I have been crowned with more glory and honor.[11] Like the soldiers who return from the battles of life to receive their stripes and pins—and the Boy Scouts and Girl Scouts with their badges and their bars—so the flaming ones who have overcome, when bidden to those formal receptions held in the retreats of the Great White Brotherhood, are required to come in full military dress. And by their dress, all know what worlds they have conquered—when and where. And old comrades who have shared in the victory of worlds reminisce in the strategy of their overcoming as they look longingly upon those now engaged in the warfare for the salvation of this planet and this people.

We who know the strategies of the dark ones would impart them to our brothers and sisters below. But the messenger who volunteered to write the book *Strategies of Darkness* took his leave in the summer of life, which leaves only the beloved Elizabeth to write oh, so many books of the law waiting on the shelves of the libraries of our retreats for the translator, the one who holds the key to decipher the Word of Spirit into the Word of Mater.

Do you know, precious ones, that these books are written in many tongues—the tongues of angels and cosmic beings and the languages that come from other systems of worlds and other interpretations of the Logos? And so we have placed the keys for the deciphering of the code in the aura of our messenger. And do you know that each of the rays of the seven archangels who are addressing you, mankind, in this series, has its own engrams of light, its own hieroglyphs of the Word? These pass through the Christ mind of our messenger and are delivered to you in the language of your understanding and in the language which the Lord God has used to deliver to mankind the teachings of the I AM in this age. Is this not truly the miracle of the science of the fifth ray? Is this not the hand of the Mother feeding her children that which they can understand and assimilate and become?

I leave you now, but only that Uriel and Aurora might fill you with the most magnificent dispensations of the archangels and the archeiai who come in the name of the Lord in this the hour of the judgment.

Mary

THE SIXTH VIAL

XI

THE JUDGMENT OF THE POLLUTION OF THE SACRED MOTHER FLOW

The Sixth Vial

Children of the One
Who Keep Your Garments in the Lord:

I am Uriel of the sixth ray
Of the dawn of Christed awareness!
Aurora stands with me
In the corona of the sun behind the sun—
Your own beloved I AM Presence.
With the golden key we unlock the mystery
Of the purple and the gold.

Look up now and behold
Rivers of waters flowing
From the center of the sun,
White fire and crystal
Sparkling from the center,
Flowing yellow, pink, and violet,
Purple, green, and blue,
Flowing from the heart of God
To you and you and you.

Your own causal body
Is the paradise of the soul.

For every creature it is creation's goal
To return to the center of the One,
To be in the flaming white-fire sun.
For this, for this, the journey of the soul:
Ascend to Alpha, Omega,
The undisputed Whole!

The Garden of Eden was created by the Lord God as a haven of light and loveliness, as a replica of the causal body for the early root races who did not depart from the perfection of the plan.[1] In the center of the garden was the Tree of Life, focus of the I AM Presence made tangible in Mater. And the tree of the knowledge of good and evil was the presence of the Christ, the blessed mediator in whose consciousness is the balance of understanding of the absolute perfection of God and the relative imperfection of man and woman. "And the Lord God commanded the man, saying, Of every tree of the garden thou mayest freely eat: but of the tree of the knowledge of good and evil, thou shalt not eat of it: for in the day that thou eatest thereof thou shalt surely die."

Eve's hearkening unto the serpent who said, "Ye shall not surely die" was the first compromise of the flame of the Christ on Terra. And so it came to pass that the generations of the fourth root race who lived in the abundance of the Motherland did partake of the energies of the Christ and of the fruit of the vine before they were initiated by Almighty God to be partakers of the Holy Communion. Later, the one who said, "I AM the vine, ye are the branches;[2] except ye eat the flesh of the Son of man and drink his blood, ye have no life in you"[3] would come to initiate mankind in the sacred energies of the Word and of the Logos. He would come to initiate the ritual whereby man and woman consecrated in Christ might partake of the Eucharist.

The penalties for seizing the fruit of the vine

before it is offered in grace from the hand of God are grave indeed. The expulsion from paradise was the sealing of the causal body from the access of fallen man and fallen woman. Their rebellion was against the law of the Christ. Thus by wrong choice, engineered in the cunning of the serpentine mind, they cut themselves off from the Lord's table and from the abundant gifts and graces that are the gnosis of the tree of knowledge. And lest their rebellion and their arrogance should cause them to put forth their hand and take also of the Tree of Life, partaking of the energies of the I AM THAT I AM and investing these in the creations of the wicked, the Lord God drove man and woman from the garden of paradise.

To guard the consciousness of the I AM THAT I AM, he placed at the east of the garden "cherubim and a flaming sword which turned every way to keep the way of the Tree of Life." The east is the side of the Christ consciousness and the sword is the sacred Word of living truth that proceeds out of the mouth of the Faithful and True. It is the sword which turns every way in the quadrants of Mater to protect the soul's outpicturization of the threefold flame of the Christed one. And the cherubim are the guardian consciousness of Almighty God who protect that flame in man and woman, in heaven and earth, in the holy of holies and in the coordinates of time and space.

I stand before the living presence of the law in each and every soul who, upon reading my words, does utter the vow of allegiance to the Tree of Life, the I AM Presence. And I read the proclamation that comes from the hand of Alpha and Omega this day. It is a proclamation of opportunity in grace for your soul to return to paradise lost, to the garden of the causal body, to the place where the consciousness of the Christ implants the knowledge of the tree of the knowledge of good and evil.

For every soul who reads these words who has entertained the consciousness of the Fall, I bring opportunity for the ascent to the throne of grace. The path of your journey to the end of the cycles of personal and planetary karma has been calculated for you and for every soul who has gone forth from the center of the sun to the periphery of the created spheres in Matter. To each and every one who does with allegiance run, the formula and the forcefield of light are given into the hand of your own beloved Christ Self.

Therefore, go not a whoring after other gods and other Christs and spirit guides with their fantasies and their filth of psychic phenomena.[4] But let every man and woman sit under his own vine and fig tree,[5] under his own Christ Self and I AM Presence, even as Jonah sat in the shadow of the gourd which the Lord God prepared to deliver him from his grief and the groaning of his soul struggling in the way of surrender.[6] Are you in that way this day? Are you, with Saul, the unredeemed, kicking against the pricks of the Christ?[7] Behold, your redemption draweth nigh![8] Behold, your Redeemer liveth![9]

I am the flaming presence of the Christed one! I stand before you, yet I am in the center of the sun! I am the living presence of the flame—mine to have and yours to claim. There is a way. It is the way of life made plain; it is the flow of the crystal-fire mist that consumes the mist-ification of the serpent mind.

Behold how the waters flow as a river out of Eden, descending to nourish the planes of Mater with the fiery flow of the energies of Spirit. And the flow of the crystal cord was parted and became into four heads.[10] And the first, Pison, compasseth the whole land of Havilah, symbolizing the etheric plane, where there is gold and bdellium and the onyx stone; and the second is Gihon that compasseth the whole land of Ethiopia, symbolizing the mental plane; and the third is Hiddekel which goeth toward Assyria, symbolizing the astral plane; and the fourth is Euphrates which stretcheth across the plains, symbolizing the watering of the entire physical plane.

Now let us see how mankind, by their misuses of the sacred fire in the sixth ray of the Lord Christ, have polluted the four streams of the consciousness of God flowing. And let us see how their own lifestreams have suffered from every extreme of flood and fire and drought and dire pestilence and pain, of tempest and tornado and the foreboding stillness before the roaring hurricane, oncoming glacier, Vesuvius' eruption, or the great tidal wave. The calamities of Mater, as elemental life[11] overthrow the misuses of the elements, break upon the back of fallen man and fallen woman: "For dust thou art, and unto dust shalt thou return."[12]

Now comes the angel of the sixth ray from out the Temple of the Tabernacle of the Testimony. And I pour forth my vial upon the great river Euphrates; and the water thereof is dried up, that the way of the kings of the East might be prepared.[13] Now hear the testimony of the sixth of the angels who deliver the golden vials of the wrath of God upon the earth.

The pouring-out of the vial of mankind's misuses of the light of the sixth ray must precede the judgment of the great whore, that perversion of the feminine ray that sitteth upon many waters. And in her fornication she has perverted the sacred Mother flow of the white-fire core in Mater. And this flow of the great river Euphrates was for the nourishment of the body of God upon earth who formed the Church of our Lord. And yet that Church is become as Babylon the great, the apostate Church that "is become the habitation of devils and the hold of every foul spirit and a cage of every unclean and hateful bird."[14]

And I am the angel who talked with John. And I

showed him that woman sitting "upon the scarlet-colored beast, full of names of blasphemy, having seven heads and ten horns," that woman "arrayed in purple and scarlet color and decked with gold and precious stones and pearls, having a golden cup in her hand full of abominations and filthiness of her fornication." And John saw the name written upon her forehead: "MYSTERY, BABYLON THE GREAT, THE MOTHER OF HARLOTS AND ABOMINATIONS OF THE EARTH." And he saw "the woman drunken with the blood of the saints and with the blood of the martyrs of Jesus."[15] And I told him that the waters which he saw where the whore sitteth, even the waters of the great river, are the peoples and multitudes and nations and tongues[16] who gave their energies to Babylon the great.

Therefore the crystal-flowing waters of the Mother, misused and misapplied, misappropriated and misaligned with the great whore, are dried up, in order that those who have the mastery of the Christ flame might come forth and take dominion over the earth. Enter the kings of the East! Enter the wise men who have exercised wise dominion in the uses of the threefold flame! These carry the abundance of the Mother which shall not be taken from them. Now let us see the judgment of Babylon the great and of these things which were foretold by Jesus the Christ which will shortly come upon mankind unless they repent of their deeds.

You who would keep your garments in the Lord as veils of innocence that are for the covering of the body of the Mother, let your gaze rest upon the stars, upon the trees that move in the winds of the Holy Spirit, upon the highest mountain your eyes can trace where you see the turning of the worlds as the clouds move into the sun.

The rending of the veil of innocence is the great

calamity of mortal existence. It was not intended that man and woman should partake of the fruit of the tree of the knowledge of good and evil prior to the initiations of the Christ. The immediate consequence of the act was that the eyes of them both were opened and they knew that they were naked and they sewed fig leaves together and made themselves aprons. This is the rending of the veil of innocence—and only the sacred fire reapplied can mend that veil—the garment of purity in which the Lord God sealed the souls who descended into Mater that they might not be contaminated by the energy veil called evil.

"And they heard the voice of the Lord God walking in the garden in the cool of the day: and Adam and his wife hid themselves from the presence of the Lord God amongst the trees of the garden."[17] Can you imagine hiding from the presence of the Lord? Yet since the expulsion from Eden, mankind have sought to deceive their God! And in so doing, they have deceived only themselves. The veils of this innocence are the veils of the seven rays worn by the bride, the Lamb's wife, who hath made herself ready, who hath prepared her consciousness for the consummation in the Christ flame, for the return to the paradise of the I AM THAT I AM. Walking hand in hand with the beloved, the Lamb of God, the Virgin Queen returns to the holy of holies and is received as the Bride of the Holy Spirit. Let the children of the One who would keep their garments come together in the hallowed circle of the AUM for the weaving of the wedding garment; for none shall come to the marriage supper of the Lamb without that garment.[18]

I am Uriel standing in the place of the sun! Centered in the great sun disc, I am come. I stand before all who have rent their garments and who know not that they are naked before the Lord God, and I say: Thou sayest, I am rich and increased with goods and have need of nothing; and knowest not that thou art wretched and miserable and poor and blind and naked: I counsel thee to buy of me the gold of the sixth ray, gold tried in the fire, that thou mayest be rich, and white raiment, the raiment of the archangels, that thou mayest be clothed and that the shame of thy nakedness do not appear; and anoint thine eyes with eyesalve, that thou mayest see the light of the holy of holies.[19]

I call to the children of the One! I contact each heart flame with the golden fire of the sun! In the name of the Lord God, I call unto Adam and to Eve: Where art thou? Where is thy consciousness? Where is thy heart? Where is thy mind and thy soul? And I demand that you give answer this day! You cannot linger in the shadows when the sun is in his zenith. Come out from the shadows and declare!

Where art thou? Who art thou? What doest thou with the sacred energies of thy God? Come out of your houses! Rise from your beds! Leave your slumbering and your tampering with the sacred fire! Listen to the words of the Spirit, the Amen, the faithful and true witness: "I know thy works, that thou art neither cold nor hot: I would thou wert cold or hot. So then because thou art lukewarm and neither cold nor hot, I will spue thee out of my mouth."[20]

Saint Germain, noble hierarch of the Aquarian age, defender of the flame of freedom in the hearts of all mankind, has spoken! And yet his words have fallen on the deafness and the dumbness of those who are more dense than the rocks themselves. Yet the Lord has said, "If these should hold their peace, the stones would immediately cry out."[21] If the children of the One will not come forward to declare their allegiance to the ascended hosts—will not feel the fervor of the love of Almighty God in this moment of cycles turning—then will elemental life rise up to defend the light of the Woman and her seed. And they will carry the flame of the Mother which others have discarded by the way.

Each time a child of God lets down that flame, the elementals who are the devotees of the Mother of the Seasons, the Mother of the Four Quadrants, leap from their chores in the garden of God to catch the torch lest it touch the ground. They will not allow the desecration of the Mother flame. They keep their garments. Therefore, confess your nakedness before your own I AM Presence, that the judgment of fallen man and fallen woman might be pronounced in the holy of holies. And then begin to cast out sin, your victory win, and enter in.

The judgments of the Lord are just and true. His mercy is the liberation of the soul. The expulsion from Eden was the justice of the law providing opportunity in time and space for man and woman to weave their seamless garment and to return to the habitation of God. And this is the promise of the Almighty One that will surely come to pass: "Behold, I come as a thief. Blessed is he that watcheth and keepeth his garments, lest he walk naked and they see his shame."[22]

I leave you with the meditations of my heart upon the Lord Christ. I seal you in the meditations of my heart, which shall be unto you a forcefield in Mater of the secret place of the Most High. Abide in the holy of holies! Abide under the shadow of the Almighty![23] Abide in the flame of the ark of the covenant, and know surcease from all sorrow under the trustful wings of the covering cherubim.

I AM

Uriel

of the dawn of light's confession
of the Word within you

XII

NOW IS THE JUDGMENT OF THIS WORLD

The Trial of the Mother and Her Children

Children of the One Who Would Drink
the Communion Cup of Our Lord:

I come as the woman with the alabaster box of ointment.[1] I come with the precious spikenard, and I break the box and I pour it upon the head of the Mother and upon the head of her children. Let the fallen ones murmur against me as I perform the ritual of the law. As Jesus defended the rite of the woman, so the Lord Christ this day does defend the right of the Mother and of the children of God to receive the anointing of an archeia: "Let her alone: against the day of my burying hath she kept this ritual."[2]

And this anointing of the crown chakra of the Mother and her children shall be reenacted by the Mother of the Flame as an initiation for devotees who enter into the holy of holies of the Church Universal and Triumphant. Therefore, those who drink the full cup of the blood of Christ and those who partake of the body of Christ will also stand before the Pontius Pilate of this world. For in order that the Luciferians might be judged, they must reenact their judgment of the Christed ones.

Let the chief priests and the elders of the people take counsel against the Mother and her children. Let them bind her and let them lead her away.[3] For this is their hour and the power of darkness.[4] Judge not, lest ye be judged.[5] And when the witnesses bear false testimony against the Mother and when they contradict themselves in their lies, the Mother will speak not a word.[6] For the word of the Logos and the two-edged sword of truth shall be unto her the defense of righteousness.

Let the Lion of the tribe of Juda come forth to defend the Mother in the hour of her deliverance from evil and the evil generation![7] Let those who betray the Mother flame do quickly that which they must do![8] The archangels make way for the betrayers, that they might betray themselves and therefore be found wanting in the judgment day.

There are many who harbor hatred and malice, lies and blasphemies against the Mother and her children. And they keep their evil secret in their hearts; and they gossip among themselves in the shadows of the marketplaces, turning away the young souls from the flame that will not be quenched, from the flame that is salvation to the creation and to every living creature. Therefore, we let the sword pierce the soul of the Mother "that the thoughts of many hearts may be revealed," that their karma may be congealed.[9] For by their word they shall be justified and by their word they shall be condemned.[10] And every man shall be judged according to his works.[11]

The crucifixion is the passion of the Lord and of the saints who have gotten the victory over the beast and over his image and over his mark and over the number of his name. And this passion is the intensification of the love fires in the hearts of the saints as they walk the sorrowful way, making it the glorious way as step by step, station by station, they fulfill the fourteen tests of the Christed ones.

The archangels and the archeiai do sponsor the children of the One as they pass through the fiery trial. Therefore we counsel: "Above all, take the shield of faith, wherewith ye shall be able to quench all the fiery darts of the wicked."[12] And the fourteen angels who keep the flame of life for the body and the soul of the Mother and her children hold the keys to the victory in the fourteen stations of the cross.

As you read our admonishments set forth in these fourteen *Pearls of Wisdom,* let them be for your strengthening as you face the Lord Christ and his Mother and her flame and the Word incarnate. And as you prepare to receive from the Holy Spirit those sacred fires that are for the consuming of all resistance of the carnal mind to the quickening of the soul through the adversity of the cross,

Stand, face, and conquer with sword in hand
and the fire of love burning in your heart!
Stand, face, and conquer the dividing of the waters
and the vials we impart!
Stand, face, and conquer! Plunge the sword of truth
into the cause and core of the lie.
Stand, face, and conquer! For the army of the Lord
draweth nigh.

Sons and daughters of God, do not turn away from your fiery destiny which is written by the angels in the Book of Life in script of gold. Remember Jesus, the beloved Son of God who, resolute in love and in passionate fervor for the will of God, resisted every temptation to turn from the path of the crucifixion. And when he told his disciples of the many things that he should suffer of the elders and chief priests and scribes and that he would be killed and raised again the third day, Peter rebuked him.[13]

Like the modern metaphysicians who in their

mentalizing avoid the confrontation of the initiation of the crucifixion, Peter declared in his carnal-mindedness, "Be it far from thee, Lord, this shall not be unto thee." Let all those who profess that the crucifixion is unnecessary yet who would be partakers of the resurrection and the ascension hear the denunciation of the Lord: "Get thee behind me, Satan: thou art an offence unto me: for thou savourest not the things that be of God, but those that be of men."

In the hour of the judgment, the Lords of Karma count the disciples of the Lord. And when you feel the intensity of the ray of the Lord upon your head, know that the examination by the Lord's emissaries is upon you and the accounting of works is being tallied by the angels of the Keeper of the Scrolls. Let us hear the formula spoken by Jesus whereby you may weigh yourself beforehand to determine what the accounting will be: "If any man will come after me, let him deny himself and take up his cross and follow me."

We shall see; we shall see who is willing to bear the cross of personal and planetary karma. We shall see who will seek to save his life and who will lose his life for the sake of the Christ. For the Son of man shall come in the glory of his Father. Your own Christ Self will descend in the glory of your own I AM Presence and with the angels of the Christed one. And then Jesus in the Christ Self of all shall reward every man according to his works.

See here now! Resist the weeping and the wailing of the daughters of Jerusalem and those that revile the sons and daughters of God who are willing to place themselves on the cross for Christ and for humanity.[14] Let them wag their heads! Let them dare you to come down from the cross! Let them have their mockery, even the thieves which "cast the same in his teeth."[15]

In that moment, blessed ones, let the meditation of the heart of a Christ be in your heart: "The cup which my Father hath given me, shall I not drink it?"[16] When the Lord is ready, he will send more than twelve legions of angels from the heart of the Father to deliver you from all evil.[17] Let deliverance come in the Lord's time, for he will extend the time and the space of the persecution of the Christed ones in order that the wicked might be judged while they hold the instruments of wickedness in their hands.

While the judgment of Almighty God is delivered unto this generation through the hand of the seven archangels, the sons and daughters of God, initiated for the crucifixion by the Mother, must hold the balance in their bodies, in their souls, in their chakras, and in their consciousness, in order that the judgment will not utterly destroy a planet and a people. For now is the judgment of this world; now is the prince of this world cast out by the fiat of Alpha and Omega. And there is a price to be paid by the sons and daughters of God for the exorcism of the Fallen One and his angels, and the price is the sacrifice of the ego.

Therefore, put down the ego, raise up the Christ, and learn the meaning of the statement of the Lord "And I, if I be lifted up from the earth, will draw all men unto me."[18] When you raise up the energies of the Christ, when you allow the fires of the Mother to rise as the caduceus on the staff of life, the light of Mother and Son magnetized in your aura will draw the souls of mankind into the presence of the Holy Spirit and into the center of the I AM THAT I AM.

Yes, there is a price to be paid. The Mother of the Flame has agreed to pay the price. Will you agree also as you walk in the way with her? Your own beloved Lanello made the announcement on the last day of 1974 that hierarchy could no longer hold back the increase of light in her body and in her soul. In order for Terra to pass through the hour of her crucifixion unto the glory of her resurrection, "the light must be increased, the light must be intensified, and the repository of that light is our messenger in form."[19] The light is increased for the salvation of souls. Yet this light, as the piercing of the sword of truth, precipitates human hatred; and upon that cross the Mother is crucified, and her children and all who take up the cross of Christ after her.

With the increase of light comes also the joy of miracles of healing dispensed unto the children through her healing hands. And in the darkest hour of the night, when the light is increased to the uttermost, when many shall be offended and shall betray one another and shall hate one another, remember the words that are written, "Then all the disciples forsook him and fled."[20] Stand staunch therefore, children of the Mother, to defend that flame when the Mother is "hated of all nations for my name's sake."[21] Let it not be written in the record of the judgment that you denied her thrice before the crowing of the cock.[22]

For Lanello has prophesied that many shall turn away from the flame of the Mother because her love will draw out the toxins of hatred from their four lower bodies, and this hatred must be extracted in order that their souls might be saved from the karma of their own hatred. Those who commit their karma unto the flame of the sacred fire before it turns to boils and sores upon their bodies will remain in the mandala of the Mother. But those who do not will blaspheme her name because of their pains, and they will not repent of their deeds.

Jesus the Christ, the true head of the Church Universal and Triumphant, extends to you the communion cup, saying "Drink ye all of it."[23] And you remember his words in Gethsemane, "Father, if thou be willing, remove this cup from me: nevertheless, not my will, but thine be done."[24] And when you have made your commitment to the will of God, the soldiers of the governor will give you the cup of vinegar mingled with gall. You will taste it, but you will not drink thereof.[25]

This is the cup of the wrath of mankind's karma which they would force the Christed ones to take. This is their cup! Let them drink it! For this is the judgment of the Lord that came through the prophet Jeremiah: "And the Lord saith, Because they have forsaken my law which I set before them and have not obeyed my voice, neither walked therein, but have walked after the imagination of their own heart and after Baalim, which their fathers taught them, therefore thus saith the Lord of hosts, the God of Israel: Behold, I will feed them, even this people, with wormwood and give them water of gall to drink. I will scatter them also among the heathen, whom neither they nor their fathers have known: and I will send a sword after them, till I have consumed them."[26]

In the pouring-out of the seven golden vials of the last plagues of mankind's karma are the wormwood and the gall given to mankind while the judgment is upon them. Enter into the holy of holies and into the white-fire core of the Mandala of the Mother. Seek refuge in the temple of the Lord and in the Church Universal and Triumphant; and there partake of the Eucharist and see how the alchemy of the Christ consciousness is performed within you by the blessed mediator.

Now is forgiveness come to those who have been the unwitting instruments of the fallen ones. Jesus forgave the people from the cross, saying, "Father, forgive them; for they know not what they do."[27] Hear then the judgment that is taken from the Book of Life! The Jews were made scapegoats for the crucifixion of the Lord. They were but instruments of the chief priests and the elders of the people. It is *they* who took counsel to put Jesus to death. These are the fallen ones, the Luciferians; and the captains and the soldiers were their robot creation. *They* used the mob to enact their murder of the Christed One, and *they* tricked the Jews into taking upon themselves the karma of the deed. Therefore in the midst of the tumult created by the fallen ones, they cried out, "His blood be on us and on our children!"[28]

I am the angel with the avenging sword! And I proclaim this day with the Lord Christ: They are exonerated of all guilt surrounding the death of Christ. And let this word be spoken in the temples of the Jews and in their synagogues—that the Mother of Christ has this day extended her hand through the Mother of the Flame to draw into the holy of holies all who are of the house of Israel. These are they who love the name of the Lord, I AM THAT I AM, and who accept their own mediator, the Christed one, as able to forgive all sin and the sense of sin.

This day is the judgment turned upon the fallen ones, and they shall bear the burden of their karma! It is they who have slain the Lamb from the foundation of the world.[29] Let the energy return to their doorstep!

Now let the children of the One see through the divide-and-conquer tactics of the wicked! Let those who call themselves Christians forgive the members of the house of David. Let all who worship the God of Israel embrace those who have followed the Messiah into the new age of the proclamation of the law of Moses and the grace of Jesus Christ.

I AM

Aurora

of the sixth ray

I bring the dawn of illumination unto the new day.

THE SEVENTH VIAL

XIII

THE JOY OF JUDGMENT IN THE FLAME OF TRANSMUTATION

The Seventh Vial

Children of the One Trusting in the Law of Freedom:

I am the angel of the seventh ray, and there is given unto me this day the seventh golden vial of the wrath of God. I pour out this vial into the air, and the great voice out of the temple of heaven is heard throughout the planes of Spirit and the planes of Mater! From the throne of the Almighty One, guarded by the four cosmic beings who stand on the side of the north and on the side of the south and on the side of the east and on the side of the west of the throne of God, is the word of the Logos pronounced: "It is done!" And as that word is translated throughout the planes of Mater, there is a trembling of many voices and thunders and lightnings.[1]

The light emanations from the center of a cosmos are emitted in rings from the center to the periphery, from Spirit unto Mater. As these rings of light, as waves of light,undulate through the great cosmic sea farther and farther from the center of the flame of the One, the energy is stepped down by cosmic hierarchies—mighty seraphim and cherubim, the Elohim and the archangels—so that in each successive frequency of Mater there is released the light necessary for the alchemicalization, the translation of darkness into light. And where there is a greater concentration of sin and the sense of sin and of separation from the One, the many voices of the heavenly hosts and the thunders and the lightnings that are the release of the sacred fire cause great earthquakes as the atoms and molecules of Mater are brought into sudden alignment with the white-fire core of the Holy Spirit.

In that hour of the judgment of the evolutions in those systems of worlds where souls have partaken of the fruit of the tree of knowledge of good and evil, men and women are hushed in anticipation of that great earthquake which has not been seen since the inhabitation of the planets. This is that cataclysm which begins within the soul as the light of the Great Central Sun arcs to the seed of man and woman for the purification of the lifestreams for the Aquarian age. The light must travel through the entire body of Mater, through your four lower bodies, through the four planes of consciousness of Terra and of the planets of this solar system.

The light is oncoming! It fills the body of God upon earth and they rejoice in the living fountain of fire. The children of the One frolic in the bubbling waters of life that flow freely from the "pure river of water of life, clear as crystal, proceeding out of the throne of God and of the Lamb."[2] They are not afraid to enter in, for they have already voluntarily consigned all misqualified substance into the violet flame. They have been washed by the waters of the Word;[3] they fear no loss of identity. They fear not the rod of the commeasurement of the Infinite One; they fear not the measuring of man and woman.

They know because they are known of God. Their names are written in the Book of Life;[4] they have fought the good fight over darkness and death.[5] They have invoked the Christ and the action of the full complement of the archangels to lay hold on the dragon of the carnal mind and to bind that usurper of the light and to set the seal of Maitreya upon the dweller on the threshold, that it no longer have any hold upon the soul ascending to the throne of God.

The violet flame is a flame of joy as it sweeps through the consciousness of humanity. Flowing with the great flow of the Holy Spirit, it frees every particle of energy that it touches. The flame caresses Mater; for the flame is the Holy Spirit that is wed to the Divine Mother, who is the white-fire core of all energy cycles. The great love of the Spirit for the Mother and of the Mother for the Spirit is the magnetism of Alpha and Omega drawing the flame of purification from on high into the canyons of the great rivers, into the crevasses of the mountains, into the nooks and crannies of the rocks. Wherever there is an opening, wherever there is an invitation, the fires of freedom roll and the angels of Zadkiel and Holy Amethyst deposit the universal solvent which throughout the ages the alchemists have sought.

When the earth is bathed in the violet flame, as after a summer rain, the elementals splash in puddles and ponds of the violet elixir which remain. The four lower bodies of a planet and a people absorb the flow of violet fire as the parched earth and the grasses dried in the summer sun absorb water. The violet flame and the violet-flame angels release a momentum that causes the electrons to spin. It is a momentum of joy! For joyousness and laughter—the kind of laughter that one has when one has gotten the victory over the self—bubble in the soul and bounce through the four lower bodies, sweeping away the debris of doubt and fear, the depressions of the years and the discarnates that lurk in the darkened corners of the mind.

Now is the acceptable time of joy. It is the joy of

the judgment! The wise elementals leap with the precision of a thousand ballerinas in formation—leap into the flame of judgment, leap into the joy of the violet fire—for they know that the judgment is the first step in their liberation and their ultimate reunion with the flame of life. There is no hesitation with the sylphs and the undines, gnomes and salamanders. They come into the fire and the fiery pools—the seven sacred pools that are for the cleansing of all life step by step from the karma of the misuse of the energies of the seven rays.

Remember Naaman, the captain of the host of the king of Syria, a mighty man of valor albeit a leper, whose servant besought him to seek the prophet of Israel to heal him of his leprosy.[6] And by and by "Naaman came with his horses and with his chariot and stood at the door of the house of Elisha. And Elisha sent a messenger unto him, saying, Go and wash in Jordan seven times, and thy flesh shall come again to thee and thou shalt be clean." And Naaman was wroth, and he turned and went away in a rage because the prophet did not come forth and with great fanfare make invocation to the Lord.

See how the carnal mind of the high and the mighty would have the prophet of the Lord do their bidding! But the servants of Naaman prevailed upon him; and he went down "and dipped himself seven times in Jordan, according to the saying of the man of God: and his flesh came again like unto the flesh of a little child, and he was clean."

Now let mankind form a queue that they might dip into the waters of the Mother, into the white-fire core of the energies of the Cosmic Virgin. And let them be cleansed seven times by the action of the fires of the seven rays. Let them be cleansed of their misuses of the seven aspects of the Logos. Let them dip seven times into the sacred pools of the Mother for the cleansing of the chakras. Let them dip seven times for the cleansing of the soul and the four lower bodies. Let them dip themselves seven times for the initiations of Lord Maitreya whereby the Holy Spirit is sealed in the chakras forevermore.

You who would be captains in the Lord's hosts, you who would have the mantle of responsibility to lead the children of God into the light and to guide the governments of the nations according to the just laws of heaven and earth, humble yourselves before the flame of the Mother! Be willing to be washed. Be willing to be washed.

The seventh ray is the ray of ceremony and ritual whereby, through the performance of these things, transmutation does take place. And there are rituals which will be required of thee. Some thou wilt understand and some thou wilt not. Nevertheless, follow the ritual of the law; meet the requirements set forth by the prophet. For the prophet does stand in the holy place to cast out the abomination of desolation from the temple of the soul. The prophet is standing in the holy place with the fire of Alpha and Omega to make you whole.

See then the fate of those who prefer the mark of the beast, of those who have chosen to fall down and worship the devil who has promised to give them all of the kingdoms of this world.[7] And for a trifle—a new house, a new car, a dishwasher, a washing machine—they have forsaken the flame of the Holy Spirit. Those who are possessive of material things or of spiritual things will not keep either. Only those who move in the flow of the Mother can enjoy the Mater-realization. Only those who flow in the movement of the Holy Spirit can know the joy of Spirit-realization.

The law of receiving and giving, giving and receiving, is the fulfillment of the circle of the AUM. Therefore, let go and let the energies of God flow if you would get the victory over the beast and over his image and over his mark and over the number of his name. If you would be free of the judgment of the fallen ones, let go! Let go and pursue God with all diligence.

Remember Gehazi, the servant of Elisha, who ran after Naaman to claim the gifts which the prophet had rejected.[8] And in his lust for material things, he lied and begged of Naaman a talent of silver and two changes of garments for the sons of the prophets. Naaman was overjoyed to receive the servant of Elisha, to be able to give the prophet a token for his healing; but the prophet was not overjoyed. He knew that no amount of earthly goods could be placed in the scale with the gift of healing God had given into his hands.

Therefore, unto Gehazi was rendered the pronouncement of the judgment, the same judgment that is rendered this day to those who have forsaken the flame of the Mother for the perversions of materialism: "The leprosy therefore of Naaman shall cleave unto thee and unto thy seed forever." And Gehazi went out from his presence a leper as white as snow.

See now how the alchemy of the seventh ray can produce the precipitation in your four lower bodies of the degradation of the Holy Spirit which you have harbored in your soul. Children of the One, invoke the violet flame day and night, that all your darkness might take flight before the coming of the judgment and the karma of the misuses of the seventh ray are upon you.

Take heed! Hear my word this day! For I am Zadkiel, and I hold in my retreat over the island of Cuba seven other vials given unto my keeping by the Lord God of hosts. These are the seven vials of the concentrated energies of the violet flame that will be poured out over the earth by the archangels of the seven rays when mankind have invoked enough of the sacred fire to warrant the release of these concentrated energies of the sacred fire.[9]

I stand on the side of the west of the City Foursquare. I stand on the West Coast of the United States of America, and I face the East and the kings and queens of the East to gather them to the battle of that great day of God Almighty. I raise my hands for the release of the momentum of the violet flame that shall reverse the tide of darkness and roll it back from the West unto the East. And it shall be as the rolling-up of a mighty scroll, and it shall be the rolling-up of that darkness which has covered the land. And it shall be the rolling-up of the unclean spirits that, like frogs, have been sent forth out of the mouth of the dragon and out of the mouth of the beast and out of the mouth of the false prophet.[10]

And the momentum of that tide of light will be the rolling-up of the spirits of the devils working miracles, impersonating the Christ when they are antichrist, impersonating the prophets of the Lord although they have blasphemed their name. And all of this shall come to pass when the children of the light and the Keepers of the Flame shall rally to the defense of the side of the west and invoke the momentum of the archangels to turn the tide of the Dark Cycle and to make the day of the Lord's judgment the day of joyousness in victory.

I make way for the coming of Holy Amethyst, who will seal the vials of the seven last plagues. For the victory I place my trust in God. For the battle of Armageddon I place my trust in the hosts of the Lord and in the sons and daughters of God who keep the flame of life on Terra.

I AM

Zadkiel

of the seventh ray of transmutation

XIV

THE INITIATION OF THE JUDGMENT

The Uses and Misuses of the Seven Rays

Children of the One Abiding in the Shadow
of the Mercy of the Law:

I am the flame of Zadkiel and the jewel in the center of the flame. I am the point of the precipitation in Mater of the alchemy of the seventh ray. I am the Mother flame of the order of Melchizedek.[1] I am the white-fire core of the seat-of-the-soul chakra. I am a keeper of the flame, keeping the flame of freedom for the seven root races destined to fulfill the cycles of life on Terra.

I stand at the south portico of our retreat over the island of Cuba. I face the children of the South, children of Mother Mary, those delicate ones who, in their humble lives and gentle adoration of the Mother, are the guardians of the light of the Christos in this hemisphere. And then I walk to the north portico where Zadkiel stands gazing upon the children of the North, who keep the flame of freedom for a planet and a people who have enshrined that flame in the name of Uncle Sam in the government and in the economy of a nation destined to be the Mother light come again.

And so in the masculine and feminine rays of

the Godhead, we distribute the energies of freedom through the amethyst crystal on the altar of our retreat. And the flame that burns here, tended by legions of violet-flame angels, sparkles with the brilliance of every tone that is contained in the spectrum of the seventh ray. From the pink-violet to the fiery blue-purple mingling with white and crystal, there is opportunity for infinite expression of the Christ flame within these sacred fires of Aquarius. And so to creativity, to the new birth, to the science of the Mother, and to the ingenuity of her sons and daughters I dedicate my release to complete the spiral of the fourteen angels who stand in the Presence of the Lord.

I would speak to you of the initiation of the judgment for those who have prepared diligently for the coming of the Lord into the temple of being. Your own soul, clothed upon with the four lower bodies, is your focus of the Temple of the Tabernacle of the Testimony. It is the forcefield given unto you in time and space wherein you bear witness of the flame, where you become a keeper of the flame, where you dedicate God's energy entrusted into your care to the fulfillment in Mater of the counterpart of your being in Spirit.

The initiation of the judgment comes to sons and daughters of God, to the children of God, and to the fallen ones simultaneously. And yet that initiation can be the necessary preparation for the resurrection and the ascension, for the birth of the soul unto immortal life; or it can be the necessary preparation for the final judgment at the Court of the Sacred Fire and the canceling-out of the soul's identity in the ritual of the second death.

Judgment is the joy of the ritual of fulfillment because it releases the creations of the children of the One into the sacred fire. It is the trial by fire wherein every man's work must be tried and man himself must be weighed in the great balance of life.[2] To each individual soul there is given a certain epoch in time and space to fulfill the flame of the Christ in the seven rays. At the end of that era of evolution, sometimes spanning hundreds of thousands of years and thousands of incarnations, the soul must give an accounting to the Lord of Being and to the law of Selfhood, and rightly so.

The first seven chapters of the Book of Genesis are a poetic overview of the uses and misuses of the sacred fire in the seven rays. In the first chapter of the creation is the recording of the fiat of the Lord God and its implementation by the Elohim in the creation of the cosmos and of the early root races—man and woman created in the image and likeness of God, sent forth to be co-creators, to take dominion in the planes of Mater.

Interspersed with this accounting is the record of the creation of animal life and of all of the living creatures—an allegorical presentation of the creation of elemental life tainted by the fact that the authors of the Book of Genesis spoke from a point of reference in relativity; for the book was written after the fall of man and woman, after the descent of consciousness from the plane of absolute good to the plane of relative good and evil. Therefore the record of the misuses of the first ray on the mental and astral planes is also included in the account. But "God saw every thing that *he* had made, and, behold, it was very good."[3] This is the etheric blueprint of the cosmos, the power of the first ray that undergirds the all of the creation.

In the second chapter of Genesis, there is the sealing of the creation in the mind of God through the second ray of illumined action. And immediately the factor of antichrist, as the mist that went up from the earth and watered the whole face of the ground, compromised the light of the Logos in man and woman.

Now the counterpart, the material creation of the male and female formed of the dust of the ground, is given. Here evolution has reached the physical plane watered by the energies of Spirit; and out of the cloven tongues of the fire of wisdom, the counterpart of man is set before him as woman. Simultaneously the tree of the knowledge of good and evil is placed in the midst of the garden, that man and woman might exercise free will to obey or not to obey, to believe or not to believe, the word of the Lord.

Thus the Divine Us, as twin flames in the white-fire core who were created in the beginning, realize their oneness in Matter as a duality of expression. While they remain in the light of the Christ, their innocence is sealed. But the record in the third chapter of Genesis deals with the uses and misuses of the flame of love; and this is where the carnal mind, personified in the serpent who typifies the Fallen One tempting the members of the fourth root race on Lemuria, presents its carnal logic. Temptation is always presented as the lie that goes against the intuition of the heart and its natural inclination toward devotion to God.

The fall of man and woman came about as the result of their abandonment of the flame of love and the logic of the heart. The misuses of the sacred fire of love were grave indeed upon Lemuria, and they spread to every corner of the earth. The mechanization of creation caused man and woman to forfeit the holy communion of love shared in the Holy Spirit. The judgment of the men and women of the fourth root race was also the judgment of love. Outside the paradise of God's consciousness, Adam and Eve are required to master the fourth ray—no longer by the alchemy of the sacred fire, but in sorrow and in shame.[4]

The white light of the Mother in the fourth ray is so intense that it arouses anger and jealousy in Cain eventuating in the desecration of the Mother. Unto

Cain and Abel it was given to keep the flame of Alpha and Omega in the white chakra, and to that end they offered burnt offerings unto the Lord. The killing of righteous Abel by Cain was the beginning of the profanation of the flame of the Mother by the children of the Mother.[5] And so the fires of the Mother were used for the multiplication of the consciousness of Cain in a degenerate humanity.

But with the coming of Seth, the Lord's replacement for the seed of Abel, men and women began once again to call upon the name of the Lord. Through the application of the law of truth in the science of the fifth ray, the generations of Adam through Seth brought forth great lights in the history of the earth—Enos and Cainan and Mahalaleel and Jared and Enoch and Methuselah and Lamech and Noah.[6] These men had the mastery of the fifth ray and therefore lived hundreds of years through its application in the science of Mater.

But the children of the fallen ones and the generations of Cain brought about the misuse of the light of the Christ in the sixth ray. Instead of service to that light and the mastery of the emotions, it is recorded in the sixth chapter of the Book of Genesis that every imagination of the thoughts of man's heart was only evil continually.[7] And in the antediluvian society there was a mingling of light and darkness, and the rebellious ones contaminated the whole earth with their laggard consciousness. But the generations of Noah were perfect in the sight of God; and therefore he instructed Noah and his sons—Shem, Ham, and Japheth—to build the ark to prepare for the coming of the judgment.[8] The sixth ray is the mastery of water, and Noah and his house kept that mastery. Therefore unto them the judgment was a blessing and the preparing of the way for a new order.

And thus the flood came as the action of the

seventh ray—of the violet flame of transmutation, the ritual of the undoing of the perverted rituals of fallen man and fallen woman. And in that period of purification, of forty days, the four planes of Mater were washed by the waters of the living Word even as Jesus reenacted the period of purification during forty days of fasting in the wilderness.[9] While the fallen ones experienced the judgment and the trial by fire as the great purging even unto the death of their four lower bodies, Noah and his family entered into the ritual of the ark whereby the energies of Spirit and Mater arc and there is that perfect communion and that perfect flow between the heart of God and the heart of son and daughter incarnate as the living Word.

As you meditate upon these seven chapters in the presence of the Holy Spirit, you will see that in every century mankind have taken the seven rays of the Logos and qualified them according to their level of attainment in the Christ consciousness. And so it is that those who would keep the flame of life in the day of judgment that is at hand, those who would return to the center of God consciousness and be allowed to pass by the flaming sword and the cherubim who keep the way of the Tree of Life, must traverse the cycles of their own uses and misuses of the seven rays.

Step by step, line by line, karma must be balanced to the right and to the left. Each individual who reads my words must know that the responsibility to balance the energies of life is the meaning of the judgment. When you determine to get back to Eden, to return to the house of the Father-Mother God, you must be willing to retrace every footstep you have taken since the descent of your soul into the planes of Mater.

The road of return has two aspects: the sorrowful way and the glorious way. It all depends upon your perspective; for the bliss of the divine reunion is experienced within—even in the moment of agony, through the dark night of the soul, and on the cross.

The sixty-ninth Psalm of David contains three cycles of twelve. In thirty-six verses David reveals the experiences of one who passed through the dark night of the soul to the full realization of the Christ consciousness. You who have determined to pass through the dark night of both the soul and the Spirit would do well to ponder the meditations of David and then to apply yourself diligently to the invocations of the sacred fire, especially to the violet flame that is the concentrated energy of the Holy Spirit in the forgiveness of sin, the righting of all wrong, and the bringing of the four lower bodies into alignment with the original blueprint of creation.

Now I seal the seven golden vials; for in the ritual of the feminine aspect of the seventh ray, it is given to me to take from the hand of the seven archangels the seven vials. They are empty now. I seal them and I return them to the cosmic being who gave them unto the seven archangels, and they shall remain in the Temple of the Tabernacle of the Testimony until all be fulfilled through the judgments of the Lord.

Long ago in the hour of the fall of Lucifer when the son of the morning defied the Almighty One and dared him to come down from his throne to judge him in his fall, he made the sign of the clenched fist in defiance of the Lord; and this has been the sign of the rebellious generation and of the fallen angels since that hour.[10] But the Almighty would not be moved; and unto the fallen ones he gave a dispensation of mercy—certain cycles in time and space as opportunity for repentance. But they would not. No, they would not.

Therefore this day in God's own time, in God's own space, judgment is meted out to the Fallen One and those who boasted to the children of God, saying: "See, we have dared the Lord and he has not responded! The Lord is silent; therefore he does not exist. Behold Lucifer and Satan; they are more powerful than the Lord God of hosts. They have dominion in the planes of Mater; fall down and worship them!" And now the answer of the Lord has come. In his season and in his cycle, the Lord has released the judgment of the fallen ones. Let all the world know that the Lord God omnipotent reigneth![11] Let the angel choirs sing the alleluia! Let the worlds rejoice! Let the stars in the heavens rejoice! Let the sons and daughters of God rejoice, for the Lord God omnipotent reigneth!

Let the Keepers of the Flame understand that the judgment of God is manifest in the four planes of Mater and in the four lower bodies of mankind. But ultimately that judgment must manifest in the soul. Thus the energies of the judgment meted out in the cycles of the years and in the fulfillment of the centuries may not always be visible or obvious to those who have followed a literal interpretation of Scripture. Although much of that which will come upon the earth will be unseen, it will be felt and heard and known by those who are close to the flame and also by those in whom the judgment is meted out. Therefore, judge not, lest ye be judged.

Now let there be rejoicing in the retreats of the ascended masters and in the focuses of their chelas! And let the waltzes of the violet flame and the rhythm of three-quarter time be the keynote of victory. Let joy in the violet flame generate more joy for the regeneration of a planet and a people. And let the youth and the young in heart of every age come together for the waltz of the flame, for the release of joy to the four lower bodies and the four planes of Mater. And let the grand march and the waltz and the polka replace the desecration of the body of the Mother and of her children through the rhythms and the unholy dancing of the fallen ones.

In the heart of every Keeper of the Flame I place a replica of the amethyst crystal of our retreat, that you might generate the joy of living and the joy of giving on Terra, that you might clear the way for the new day and the new order of the ages and for the coming of the seventh root race, that through you the archangels might charge the governments and the economies of the nations and all cultural and educational institutions with the momentum of the new birth of the Spirit and with the momentum of light that comes forth from the Great Central Sun.

It is time to light the torch of the age of freedom. The taper is in my hand. Will you light a taper of your own and ignite the hearts of mankind to the victory of the throne, the three-in-one, the grace of Faith and Hope and Charity in the balance of life's energy? The threefold flame is calling, calling mankind home! To the victory of freedom in Terra I dedicate my flame and the release of the judgment at the hand of the seven archangels. Let judgment be for the victory of the souls of God in the dark night of the soul, for the victory of the sons and daughters of God in the initiations of the seven rays.

I set my seal upon the fire and upon the air, upon the waters and upon the earth. And I stand with Zadkiel on the west side of the city, waiting for the moment of the rolling-up of the darkness into the scroll. And when the hour is come that is signified by the Lord, the seven archangels will take that scroll of human consciousness and human creation and hand it to the Keeper of the Scrolls, who will place it in the sacred fire for the consuming of the cause, effect, record, and memory of the misuse of the sacred fire in the planes of Mater.

I AM your Mother of freedom forevermore,

Amethyst

Lord Michael

In the name of the beloved mighty victorious Presence of God, I AM in me, my very own beloved Holy Christ Self, Holy Christ Selves of all mankind, beloved Archangel Michael, beloved Lanello, the entire Spirit of the Great White Brotherhood and the World Mother, I decree:

1. Lord Michael, Lord Michael,
   I call unto thee:
   Wield thy sword of blue flame
   And now cut me free.

Refrain: Blaze God-power, protection
   Now into my world,
   Thy banner of faith
   Above me unfurl;
   Transcendent blue lightning
   Now flash through my soul,
   I AM by God's mercy
   Made radiant and whole!

2. Lord Michael, Lord Michael,
   I love thee, I do;
   With all thy great faith
   My being imbue.

3. Lord Michael, Lord Michael
   And legions of blue,
   Come seal me, now keep me
   Faithful and true.

Coda: I AM with thy blue flame
   Now full-charged and blest,
   I AM now in Michael's
   Blue-flame armor dressed! (3x)

And in full faith I consciously accept this manifest, manifest, manifest (3x) right here and now with full power, eternally sustained, all-powerfully active, ever expanding, and world enfolding until all are wholly ascended in the light and free! Beloved I AM, beloved I AM, beloved I AM!

Beloved Surya

Beloved mighty victorious Presence of God, I AM in me, my very own beloved Holy Christ Self, Holy Christ Selves of all mankind, beloved Surya, legions of white fire and blue lightning from Sirius, the Four and Twenty Elders and the Lords of Karma, beloved Saint Germain and the Great Divine Director, the seven mighty Elohim, the seven beloved archangels and the seven beloved chohans of the rays, beloved Lanello, the entire Spirit of the Great White Brotherhood and the World Mother: In thy name, by and through the magnetic power of the immortal, victorious threefold flame of truth within my heart and the heart of God in the Great Central Sun, I decree:

1. Out from the sun flow thy dazzling bright
   Blue-flame ribbons of flashing diamond light!
   Serene and pure is thy love,
   Holy radiance from God above!

Refrain: Come, come, come, Surya dear,
By thy flame dissolve all fear;
Give to each one security
In the bonds of purity;
Flash and flash thy flame through me,
Make and keep me ever free!

2. Surya dear, beloved one
   From the mighty central sun,
   In God's name to thee we call:
   Take dominion over all!

3. Out from the heart of God you come,
   Serving to make us now all one—
   Wisdom and honor do you bring,
   Making the very soul to sing!

4. Surya dear, beloved one,
   From our faith then now is spun
   Victory's garment of invincible gold,
   Our soul's great triumph to ever uphold!

And in full faith . . .

Note: This decree is mentioned by Archeia Hope on page 54.

Introit to the Holy Christ Flame

In the name of the beloved mighty victorious Presence of God, I AM in me, my very own beloved Holy Christ Self, Holy Christ Selves of all mankind, the seven beloved archangels, beloved Lanello, the entire Spirit of the Great White Brotherhood and the World Mother and through the magnetic power of the sacred fire vested within the threefold flame of love, wisdom, and power burning within my heart, I decree:

1. Holy Christ Self above me,
Thou balance of my soul,
Let thy blessed radiance
Descend and make me whole.

Refrain: Thy flame within me ever blazes,
Thy peace about me ever raises,
Thy love protects and holds me,
Thy dazzling light enfolds me.
I AM thy threefold radiance,
I AM thy living presence
Expanding, expanding, expanding now.

2. Holy Christ flame within me,
Come, expand thy triune light;
Flood my being with the essence
Of the pink, blue, gold, and white.

3. Holy lifeline to my Presence,
Friend and brother ever dear,
Let me keep thy holy vigil,
Be thyself in action here.

And in full faith I consciously accept this manifest, manifest, manifest (3x) right here and now with full power, eternally sustained, all-powerfully active, ever expanding, and world enfolding until all are wholly ascended in the light and free! Beloved I AM, beloved I AM, beloved I AM!

Flame of Healing

Beloved mighty victorious Presence of God, I AM in me, O thou beloved immortal victorious threefold flame of eternal truth within my heart, Holy Christ Selves of all mankind, beloved Helios and Vesta, beloved Hilarion, Pallas Athena, Archangel Raphael and the healing angels, beloved Jesus the Christ, Mother Mary, the Maha Chohan, beloved mighty Cyclopea and Lady Master Meta, the seven mighty Elohim, the seven beloved archangels, and the seven beloved chohans of the rays, beloved Lanello, the entire Spirit of the Great White Brotherhood and the World Mother: In the name of the Presence of God which I AM and through the magnetic power of the sacred fire vested in me, I decree:

1. Healing flame of brightest green,
I AM God Presence all serene,
Through me pour thy mercy light,
Now let truth make all things right.

Refrain: Flame of consecration wonder,
Let my mind on thee now ponder
Service to my brother stronger
And the fullness of thy power.
Flame of consecration healing,
Keep my being full of healing,
Mercy to my brothers sealing
By the grace of God-desire.

2. Flame of healing, fill my form,
Vibrant life in me reborn;
God within me, make me whole,
I AM healing every soul.

And in full faith I consciously accept this manifest, manifest, manifest (3x) right here and now with full power, eternally sustained, all-powerfully active, ever expanding, and world enfolding until all are wholly ascended in the light and free! Beloved I AM, beloved I AM, beloved I AM!

The Law of Forgiveness

Beloved mighty victorious Presence of God, I AM in me, beloved Holy Christ Self, beloved heavenly Father, beloved Great Karmic Board, beloved Kwan Yin, Goddess of Mercy, beloved Lanello, the entire Spirit of the Great White Brotherhood and the World Mother: In the name and by the power of the Presence of God which I AM and by the magnetic power of the sacred fire vested in me, I call upon the law of forgiveness and the violet transmuting flame for each transgression of thy law, each departure from thy sacred covenants. Restore in me the Christ mind, forgive my wrongs and unjust ways, make me obedient to thy code, let me walk humbly with thee all my days. In the name of the Father, the Mother, the Son, and the Holy Spirit, I decree for all whom I have ever wronged and for all who have ever wronged me:

Violet fire,* enfold us! (3x)
Violet fire, hold us! (3x)
Violet fire, set us free! (3x)

I AM, I AM, I AM surrounded by
a pillar of violet flame,*
I AM, I AM, I AM abounding in
pure love for God's great name,
I AM, I AM, I AM complete
by thy pattern of perfection so fair,
I AM, I AM, I AM God's radiant flame
of love gently falling through the air.

Fall on us! (3x)
Blaze through us! (3x)
Saturate us! (3x)

And in full faith I consciously accept this manifest, manifest, manifest (3x) right here and now with full power, eternally sustained, all-powerfully active, ever expanding, and world enfolding until all are wholly ascended in the light and free! Beloved I AM, beloved I AM, beloved I AM!

* "Mercy's flame" and "purple flame" should be used the second and third times the decree is given.

I AM the Violet Flame

In the name of the beloved mighty victorious Presence of God, I AM in me, and my very own beloved Holy Christ Self, I call to beloved Alpha and Omega in the heart of God in our Great Central Sun, beloved Saint Germain, beloved Portia, beloved Archangel Zadkiel, beloved Holy Amethyst, beloved mighty Arcturus and Victoria, beloved Kwan Yin, Goddess of Mercy, beloved Oromasis and Diana, beloved Mother Mary, beloved Jesus, beloved Omri-Tas, ruler of the violet planet, beloved Great Karmic Board, beloved Lanello, the entire Spirit of the Great White Brotherhood and the World Mother to expand the violet flame within my heart, purify my four lower bodies, transmute all misqualified energy I have ever imposed upon life, and blaze mercy's healing ray throughout the earth, the elementals, and all mankind and answer this my call infinitely, presently, and forever:

I AM the violet flame
  In action in me now
I AM the violet flame
  To light alone I bow
I AM the violet flame
  In mighty cosmic power
I AM the light of God
  Shining every hour
I AM the violet flame
  Blazing like a sun
I AM God's sacred power
  Freeing every one

And in full faith I consciously accept this manifest, manifest, manifest (3x) right here and now with full power, eternally sustained, all-powerfully active, ever expanding, and world enfolding until all are wholly ascended in the light and free! Beloved I AM, beloved I AM, beloved I AM!

Notes

Chapter I

1. 2 Cor. 6:2.
2. Rev. 15:6-7.
3. Gen. 2:9, 16-17; 3:1-7.
4. Rev. 4:4.
5. Rev. 4:5; 5:6.
6. Matt. 5:18.
7. Rev. 15:8.
8. Rev. 16:1.
9. The Dark Cycle of the return of mankind's karma began on April 23, 1969. It is a period when man's misqualified energy, held in abeyance for many centuries, is being released for balance in this period of transition into the Aquarian cycle. According to the cycles of the cosmic clock, the misqualified energies of mankind's karma were released under the hierarchy of Capricorn in the first year and in subsequent years under the hierarchies of Aquarius, Pisces, Aries, Taurus, and Gemini. April 23, 1975, commenced the seventh year of the Dark Cycle under the hierarchy of Cancer. Subsequent years are under the hierarchies of Leo, Virgo, Libra, Scorpio, and Sagittarius, at which time the cycle will recommence with Capricorn. This means that each year the respective hierarchies release the light whereby mankind may redeem the energies misused in past cycles when they have failed the initiations of that particular hierarchy. See Decree 6.04 in *Invocations and Decrees for Keepers of the Flame,* published by The Summit Lighthouse, for the ascended masters working with the twelve hierarchies, the God-qualities of their cosmic consciousness, and their perversions.
10. Rev. 15:2.
11. Exod. 3:14.
12. Rev. 4:8.
13. Alpha's dictation, "The Judgment: The Sealing of the Lifewaves throughout the

Galaxy," given July 5, 1975, at Shasta 1975, is published in the Cassette Album A7524 and in the book *The Great White Brotherhood in the Culture, History, and Religion of America* by Elizabeth Clare Prophet, published by The Summit Lighthouse.

14. Rev. 11:3.
15. Rev. 2:11; 20:6, 14; 21:8.
16. Rev. 12:10.
17. Rev. 16:2.
18. The decree is the most powerful of all applications to the Godhead. It is the command of the son or daughter of God made in the name of the I AM Presence and the Christ for the will of the Almighty to come into manifestation as above, so below. It is the means whereby the kingdom of God becomes a reality here and now through the power of the spoken Word. It may be short or long and usually is marked by a formal preamble and a closing, or acceptance. An explanation of decrees and how they work is given in *The Science of the Spoken Word* by Mark and Elizabeth Prophet, published by The Summit Lighthouse. A complete selection of decrees and songs is available in *Invocations and Decrees for Keepers of the Flame* and *The Summit Lighthouse Book of Songs*.
19. Rev. 8:4.
20. Rev. 21:16.

Chapter II

1. Rev. 12:1.
2. Rev. 12:7-8.
3. The body of Jesus was placed in the tomb shortly before sundown Friday and it was resurrected at dawn Sunday. The thirty-six hours which transpired during his soul's initiation is therefore equal to three cycles (one cycle is equal to twelve hours) on the cosmic clock, not three days.
4. Matt. 27:55-56, 61; 28: 1-9.
5. Exod. 17:11-13.
6. Isa. 40:31.
7. John 14:18.
8. Rev. 15:3.
9. Gen. 28:11-12.
10. Rev. 15:3-4.
11. Eph. 6:17.
12. Matt. 13:24-30, 36-43.
13. Rev. 19:11, 14.
14. Eph. 6:11.
15. Exod. 32:7-8.
16. Num. 21:8-9.
17. Alpha, "The Judgment."

Chapter III

1. Prov. 4:7-9.
2. Rev. 16:3.
3. Pss. 23:4.
4. John 8:44.
5. Prov. 16:22.
6. Gen. 2:6.
7. Ezek. 1:4.
8. There are fourteen scenes of the last hours of Jesus' life which represent his mastery and sacrifice on behalf of mankind. They are called the fourteen stations of the cross and signify the initiation of the crucifixion, which is passed both on an individual and planetary basis, according to the law of cycles. First station: Jesus is condemned to death; second station: Jesus is made to bear his cross; third station: Jesus falls the first

time; fourth station: Jesus meets his afflicted mother; fifth station: Simon the Cyrenian helps Jesus; sixth station: Veronica wipes the face of Jesus; seventh station: Jesus falls the second time; eighth station: Jesus consoles the holy women; ninth station: Jesus falls the third time; tenth station: Jesus is stripped of his garments; eleventh station: Jesus is nailed to the cross; twelfth station: Jesus dies on the cross; thirteenth station: Jesus is taken down from the cross; fourteenth station: Jesus is laid in the sepulcher.

9. Acts 2:3.
10. Rev. 13:10.
11. Rev. 13:10.
12. Matt. 7:15.
13. Apollo's dictation, "An Increment of Light from the Holy Kumaras," given July 6, 1975, at Shasta 1975, is published in the Cassette Album A7524 and in the book *The Great White Brotherhood in the Culture, History, and Religion of America* by Elizabeth Clare Prophet, published by The Summit Lighthouse.
14. Prov. 1:7.
15. Refers to mankind's misqualification of the pure energies that flow from the I AM Presence over the crystal cord to the lifestream, or soul, evolving in Matter.
16. Matt. 21:12-13.

Chapter IV

1. Rev. 19:16.
2. Matt. 22:37.
3. Rev. 3:20.
4. Rev. 3:1.
5. Rev. 16:14, 16.
6. Matt. 23:37-39.
7. Gen. 6:3.
8. Alpha, "The Judgment."

Chapter V

1. Luke 24:32.
2. Luke 21:26.
3. Rev. 16:4.
4. Rev. 16:5-6.
5. Rev. 16:7.
6. Exod. 7-12.
7. Isa. 53:3.
8. Rev. 19:7-9.
9. John 1:5.
10. 1 Pet. 5:8.
11. Rev. 12:9.
12. Rev. 20:3.
13. Eph. 6:12.
14. Gen. 19:24-25.
15. Gen. 3.
16. Matt. 24:15; Dan. 9:27; 11:31; 12:11.
17. Matt. 22:13.

Chapter VI

1. Matt. 24:28.
2. Rev. 12:4.
3. Rev. 17:1; 19:2.
4. Sanskrit terms for currents of wisdom, power, and love, emanating from the white-fire core of the base-of-the-spine chakra, which flow in and around the spinal altar.
5. Isa. 54:5.
6. Luke 1:38.
7. Rev. 21:2, 10.
8. 1 Sam. 4:3; Heb. 9:4.
9. Heb. 9:5.
10. Gen. 11:1-9.

Chapter VII

1. Matt. 7:14.
2. John 14:2.

3. Luke 2:34.
4. Gen. 7:11; 8:2.
5. *The Lost Books of the Bible* (Cleveland and New York: World Publishing Co., 1926), The Gospel of the Birth of Mary II; III:1-7.
6. Luke 1:11-20.
7. Luke 1:26-38.
8. 1 Cor. 15:52-53.
9. 1 Cor. 15:54-57.
10. Rev. 16:8-9.
11. Exod. 14:13.
12. Ezek. 33:11.
13. Exod. 19:16.
14. 2 Cor. 6:14.
15. Matt. 10:6.
16. 1 Cor. 15:58.
17. Rev. 3:11; 22:7, 12.

Chapter VIII

1. Gen. 3:24.
2. Luke 9:62.
3. Rev. 6:16-17.
4. Phil. 3:14.
5. Mary's Scriptural Rosary for the New Age, dictated by Mother Mary to Elizabeth Clare Prophet, is published in the Cassette Album A7326 and in the book *My Soul Doth Magnify the Lord!*, Revelations of Mary the Mother of Jesus to the Messengers Mark and Elizabeth Prophet, published by The Summit Lighthouse.
6. Eccles. 3:1-4.
7. See p. 111. See also Decree 10.13 in *Invocations and Decrees for Keepers of the Flame,* published by The Summit Lighthouse.
8. Rom. 3:8.
9. Prov. 16:25.
10. Mal. 4:2.
11. Exod. 11:4-5; Rev. 16: 3-4.
12. Job 9:10-12.

Chapter IX

1. Gen. 19:26.
2. 2 Cor. 6:17.
3. Josh. 24:15.
4. Rev. 16:10-11.
5. John 10:11.
6. Mark 14:32-42.
7. John 8:32.
8. Matt. 24:6.
9. Matt. 8:20.
10. Pss. 139:7-10.
11. In his dictation, "A Report to the Lords of Karma," given to Keepers of the Flame on February 2, 1975, at the Motherhouse in Santa Barbara, California, the Great Divine Director appealed to Keepers of the Flame to make the following call with every decree for the balancing of critical planetary energies and world karma: "In the name of the Christ, I call to the Great Divine Director and the Lords of Karma for the arresting of the spirals of darkness, of deceit, of self-deception, and of the betrayal of the Christ in America and in every nation upon earth."
12. "The Judgment of Abortion and the Abortionist," given March 10, 1974; see *Exhortations out of the Ark of the Covenant,* No. 3, published by The Summit Lighthouse.
13. Josh. 10:12-14.

Chapter X

1. Rom. 8:22-23.
2. Matt. 2:16-18.
3. Matt. 2:13.
4. John 1:14.
5. The experiences of the soul of Mary on earth are recounted in *My Soul Doth*

Magnify the Lord! by Mark and Elizabeth Prophet, published by The Summit Lighthouse. Also included are Fourteen Letters from a Mother to Her Children, Eight Mysteries of the Rosary, and Fourteen Messages.

6. Luke 2:35.
7. 2 Pet. 1:10.
8. Heb. 10:9.
9. James 2:19.
10. Matt. 17:2.
11. Pss. 8:5; Heb. 2:9.

Chapter XI

1. For an explanation of the first root races and the Fall of Man, see pp. 55-74 of *Climb the Highest Mountain* by Mark and Elizabeth Prophet, published by The Summit Lighthouse.
2. John 15:5.
3. John 6:53.
4. Exod. 34:15.
5. Mic. 4:4.
6. Jon. 4:6.
7. Acts 9:5.
8. Luke 21:28.
9. Job 19:25.
10. Gen. 2:10-14.
11. Elementals are beings of earth, air, fire, and water; nature spirits who are the servants of God and man in the planes of Matter for the establishment and maintenance of the physical plane as the platform for the soul's evolution. Elementals who serve the fire element are called salamanders; those who serve the air element are called sylphs; those who serve the water element are called undines; those who serve the earth element are called gnomes. See "God in Nature," chapter 7 of *Climb the Highest Mountain* by Mark and Elizabeth Prophet.
12. Gen. 3:19.
13. Rev. 16:12.
14. Rev. 18:2.
15. Rev. 17:3-6.
16. Rev. 17:15.
17. Gen. 3:8.
18. Matt. 22:11-12.
19. Rev. 3:17-18.
20. Rev. 3:14.
21. Luke 19:40.
22. Rev. 16:15.
23. Pss. 91:1.

Chapter XII

1. Mark 14:3.
2. John 12:7.
3. Matt. 27:1-2.
4. Luke 22:53.
5. Matt. 7:1.
6. Matt. 27:14.
7. Rev. 5:5.
8. John 13:27.
9. Luke 2:35.
10. Matt. 12:37.
11. Rev. 20:13.
12. Eph. 6:16.
13. Matt. 16:21-27.
14. Luke 23:27-28.
15. Matt. 27:38-44.
16. John 18:11.
17. Matt. 26:53.
18. John 12:32.
19. Lanello, *The Crown of the World Mother for 1975* (Cassette Recording B7509, The Summit Lighthouse, Colorado Springs, 1975).
20. Matt. 24:10; 26:56.
21. Matt. 24:9.
22. Matt. 26:75.
23. Matt. 26:27.
24. Luke 22:42.
25. Matt. 27:34.
26. Jer. 9:13-16.
27. Luke 23:34.

28. Matt. 27:25.
29. Rev. 13:8.

Chapter XIII

1. Rev. 16:17-18.
2. Rev. 22:1.
3. Eph. 5:26.
4. Rev. 20:12, 15.
5. 2 Tim. 4:7.
6. 2 Kings 5:1-19.
7. Matt. 4:8.
8. 2 Kings 5:20-27.
9. On July 3, 1976, at Higher Consciousness in Washington, D.C., Archangel Zadkiel and Holy Amethyst announced the release of the concentrated energies of the violet flame of these seven other vials for the transmutation of the seven last plagues. See Cassette Album A7650, published by The Summit Lighthouse.
10. Rev. 16:13.

Chapter XIV

1. Pss. 110:4; Heb. 5:6.
2. 1 Cor. 3:13.
3. Gen. 1:31.
4. Gen. 3:16-19.
5. Gen. 4:8.
6. Gen. 5.
7. Gen. 6:5.
8. Gen. 6:8-14.
9. Gen. 7:4; Matt. 4:1-2.
10. Isa. 14:12.
11. Rev. 19:6.

THE SEVEN RAYS AND THE SEVEN CHAKRAS

Seven Rays of the Flames Magnetized on the Seven Days of the Week	**God-Qualities Amplified through Invocation to the Flame**	**Chakras, or Centers: Chalices of Light Sustaining the Frequencies of the Seven Rays in the Four Lower Bodies**
First Ray Will of God (Blue) Magnified on Tuesday	Omnipotence, perfection, protection, faith, desire to do the will of God through the power of the Father	Throat (Blue)
Second Ray Wisdom of God (Yellow) Magnified on Sunday	Omniscience, understanding, illumination, desire to know God through the mind of the Son	Crown (Yellow)
Third Ray Love of God (Pink) Magnified on Monday	Omnipresence, compassion, charity, desire to be God in action through the love of the Holy Spirit	Heart (Pink)
Fourth Ray Purity of God (White) Magnified on Friday	Purity, wholeness, desire to know and be God through purity of body, mind, and soul through the consciousness of the Divine Mother	Base of the Spine (White)
Fifth Ray Science of God (Green) Magnified on Wednesday	Truth, healing, constancy, desire to precipitate the abundance of God through the immaculate concept of the Holy Virgin	Third Eye (Green)
Sixth Ray Peace of God (Purple and Gold) Magnified on Thursday	Ministration of the Christ, desire to be in the service of God and man through the mastery of the Christ	Solar Plexus (Purple and Gold)
Seventh Ray Freedom of God (Violet) Magnified on Saturday	Freedom, ritual, transmutation, transcendence, desire to make all things new through the application of the laws of Alchemy	Seat of the Soul (Violet)

AND THE BEINGS WHO ENSOUL THEM

Chohans, or Lords, Focusing the Christ Consciousness of the Ray; Location of Their Retreats	**Archangels and Divine Complements Focusing the Solar Consciousness of the Ray; Location of Their Retreats**	**Elohim and Divine Complements Focusing the God Consciousness of the Ray; Location of Their Retreats**
El Morya Darjeeling, India	**Michael** **Faith** Banff and Lake Louise, Canada	**Hercules** **Amazonia** Half Dome, Sierra Nevada, California, U.S.A.
Lanto Grand Teton, Teton Range, Wyoming, U.S.A.	**Jophiel** **Christine** South of the Great Wall near Lanchow, North Central China	**Apollo** **Lumina** Western Lower Saxony, Germany
Paul the Venetian Southern France	**Chamuel** **Charity** St. Louis, Missouri, U.S.A.	**Heros** **Amora** Lake Winnipeg, Canada
Serapis Bey Luxor, Egypt	**Gabriel** **Hope** Between Sacramento and Mount Shasta, California, U.S.A.	**Purity** **Astrea** Near Gulf of Archangel, southeast arm of White Sea, Russia
Hilarion Crete, Greece	**Raphael** **Mother Mary** Fatima, Portugal	**Cyclopea** **Virginia** Altai Range where China, Siberia, and Mongolia meet, near Tabun Bogdo
Nada Saudi Arabia	**Uriel** **Aurora** Tatra Mountains south of Cracow, Poland	**Peace** **Aloha** Hawaiian Islands
Saint Germain Transylvania, Romania Table Mountain in Teton Range, Wyoming, U.S.A.	**Zadkiel** **Amethyst** Cuba	**Arcturus** **Victoria** Near Luanda, Angola, Africa

INDEX OF SCRIPTURE

INDEX

What Is The Summit Lighthouse?

The Summit Lighthouse was founded in Washington, D.C., in 1958 by the Ascended Master El Morya of Darjeeling, India, for the express purpose of publishing the teachings of the ascended masters dictated to the Messengers Mark and Elizabeth Prophet. A unique nondenominational religious and philosophical organization, The Summit Lighthouse has become a forum for the ascended masters and their students throughout the world. With international headquarters in Malibu, California, and study groups and teaching centers in the major cities, the ascended masters and their students are disseminating the ancient wisdom to every nation.

From its inception, The Summit Lighthouse has remained dedicated first to the development of the unlimited spiritual potential of man, and second, to the bringing forth of such progressive revelation as will assist the individual to unfold his character, his ideals, and his understanding of cosmic law. The Summit Lighthouse seeks the betterment of mankind and the resolving of all human problems through its program of assisting individuals and nations to realize their intrinsic worth and capability.

Recognizing dogma and narrowness of belief as confining to the progress of the soul, the ascended masters' teachings point to truth wherever it is found. In their approach to the religious quest, they outline the need for reason and order as well as consecration. The writings of the great masters published by The Summit Lighthouse point to the fact that nothing happens by chance, but everything happens according to natural and spiritual laws which may often appear as chance. The universe was set into motion by Infinite Law and Infinite Wisdom. Even its finite characteristics show the scientific accuracy behind the manifestation.

The teachings of the ascended masters are available to all no matter what their educational or religious background. They are intended for those who maintain an open mind, for those who realize that a college or a high school diploma by no means marks the completion of one's study of life. Life is ongoing by nature, noble by intent, and spirited by vital purpose. Life is the great teacher of all men, and none dare close the mind to its secrets. The illusions of the world are screens that blur reality and conceal its grand design even from the most learned. Man dare not, if he would be free to know the truth, allow himself to remain sheltered by concepts that defy review, that stand idly by while civilization crumbles.

Civilized man need not tear down the systems of the past by violent revolution, for he is capable of assessing social problems and of evolving solutions without destroying those foundations which are needed to support change in every area of living. With faith in man's inherent ability to apply himself to the will of his Creator, we can seek a better understanding of ourselves and of our raison d'être here on earth.

Men need to rely on the balance wheel that nature has placed within the psyche of man. Reliance on one's own sensitivity to truth and to reality will help the individual to clear the decks of mortal illusions and release the consciousness from stabbing confusion that numbs the brain and being of man.

We are living in a time when the media are often controlled, education is sometimes biased, and prejudice is frequently incited. Each man seeks the good life, but seldom is he sure of just what good life really is. Evil forces are bent on the overthrow of all religion, right or wrong. They would like to drown its meaning in the tide of events and in the crosscurrents of social unrest. Men are willing to forfeit freedom while they place their hopes in the group mystique whose collective deliberations have been pronounced superior to individual conscience.

Midst the confusion of the age, The Summit Lighthouse rises as a spiritual tower to keep the flame of wonder, joy, and faith forever alive in the hearts of men. Its authority is derived from the order of devotees comprised of the ascended masters and their unascended chelas known as the Great White Brotherhood. Having mastered time and space and ascended into the white light of the Presence of God, the ascended masters have fostered the exploration of reality and the defining of individual self-mastery since the dawn of civilization.

This spiritual order has been behind every constructive endeavor that has ever been brought forth upon the planet. Its members have founded churches, fraternities, governments, hospitals, schools, and every type of philanthropic organization. Working in the main behind the scenes, they have mercifully overlooked mankind's violence, selfishness, and greed, always striving to replace chaos with noble purpose and actively seeking to elevate the consciousness of mankind by reestablishing man's faith in his immortal destiny as a son of God. These selfless servants have sought no personal credit for their doings. They have aligned themselves with the Presence of Life in all men as it was revealed by Jesus and others who have been sent to bring the light of truth to a darkened world.

Since its founding in 1958, The Summit Lighthouse has remained "a pillar of fire by night, a cloud by day" to all who seek the truth of the inner Self and the knowledge of cosmic law and its personal and planetary application. In the midst of the multifaceted activities of the ascended masters and the expansion of the organization under the capable direction of the messengers, The Summit Lighthouse has remained, in the words of Longfellow,

> Steadfast, serene, immovable, the same
> Year after year, through all the silent night
> Burns on for evermore that quenchless flame,
> Shines on that inextinguishable light!

The organizational requirements of an expanding movement have been met by the ascended masters in the founding of Church Universal and Triumphant, Summit University, Montessori International, and the opening of community teaching centers throughout the world. But The Summit Lighthouse endures—the tower of power upon the rock, symbol of the light of the I AM THAT I AM and the summit of each one's being, the very present help in time of trouble. To thousands of devotees of truth, The Summit Lighthouse has been a beacon through the night, guiding the soul to the port of reality.

Our standard is commitment to cosmic purpose and to the brotherhood of man under the fatherhood of God. Those whose loyalties are the same will find much in common with our service. All truth has its origin in universal law. The consciousness of man, as a repository of truth, provides opportunity for endless research. Those who study with us learn how they can overcome deep-seated limitations that, in some cases, from birth onward have prevented their manifestation of the full and rich life they were intended to enjoy.

Man is like a flower. His consciousness and body temple provide him with a platform for magnificent achievement. He is intended to blossom and to bear fruit. He is intended to pursue happiness while being harmless. He is intended to achieve, to overcome difficulties and limitations, and to rise to heights far above his present norm that he might benefit his fellowmen and set an example for the age.

If you are among those who keep an open mind and who are eager to learn new and scientific truths, keys that will unlock your full potential and free you from a sense of drudgery and frustration, if you are looking for a more effective means to help your family and friends and at the same time discover your inner Self, if you believe there is a purpose to life—that the spark was not intended to go out—then we invite you to take advantage of facts and findings that you may have never imagined could be true or possible.

Since 1958, The Summit Lighthouse has published the weekly letters of the ascended masters to their students throughout the world. Called Pearls of Wisdom, these letters are the intimate contact, heart to heart, between the Guru and the chela. They contain instruction on cosmic law, commentary on current conditions on earth, and whatever the hierarchy of the Great White Brotherhood deems necessary to the individual initiation of those who form a part of this great movement of light-bearers on earth.

The Keepers of the Flame Fraternity is a worthy body of men and women dedicated to self-improvement and the upliftment of humanity. Receipt of monthly lessons that provide graded instruction in cosmic law and the opportunity of attending special classes are among the many advantages of membership.

We welcome you to write or call us for further information about the activities of students of the ascended masters in your area. And we look forward to meeting you at our services and retreats.

Summit University Press®

BOOKS IN PRINT

Climb the Highest Mountain

Studies of the Human Aura

Intermediate Studies of the Human Aura

The Great White Brotherhood in the Culture, History, and Religion of America

Studies in Alchemy

Intermediate Studies in Alchemy

The Chela and the Path

Cosmic Consciousness as the highest expression of Heart

My Soul Doth Magnify the Lord!

The Greater Way of Freedom

Liberty Proclaims

Quietly Comes the Buddha

Prayer and Meditation

Understanding Yourself

Dossier on the Ascension

Prophecy for the 1980s

Spoken by Elohim

The Mechanization Concept

A Prophecy of Karma to Earth and Her Evolutions

The Soulless One: Cloning a Counterfeit Creation

The Martyrdom of an Empress

The Sacred Adventure

Forget Me Not

The Human Aura